Skyline 5

Workbook

Barbara Garside

MACMILLAN

Contents

Unit 1 The 20th century

1 Culture

1 Word work: words and phrases about culture

Complete the sentences with one of these words. Use a dictionary to help you.

> cultural   ~~cultural desert~~   cultural identity   culture shock   cultured   youth culture

1 This town is a <u>cultural desert</u>........... . There's just nothing to do.

2 She enjoys .... activities.

3 When I first arrived in Thailand, I had real ....

4 He is a very .... person.

5 A lot of people from ethnic minorities are concerned about losing their ....

6 The behavior and attitudes of young people is known as ....

2 Pronunciation work: word stress

a **Look at these sentences and underline the stressed syllable in the pairs of words.**

1 a) They are making good *progress* with their English.

   b) This piece of work is *progressing* well.

2 a) Have you almost finished that *project*?

   b) These are the *projected* figures for next year.

3 a) The video cassettes were *exported*.

   b) These CDs are for *export* only.

4 a) You should be careful about personal *insults*.

   b) The film *insulted* our intelligence.

5 a) Our company *imports* clothing from the Far East.

   b) The level of *imports* into the country has risen.

b **Now practice saying the sentences to yourself so you can hear the difference.**

> **Language note**
>
> Remember that some two-syllable words change their stress pattern depending on their part of speech:
> *They made their first **rec**ord in 1965.*
> *It was re**cord**ed in a studio.*

3 Skills work: reading

a Look at the title of this article. What do you think it is about?
Read through the article quickly to check your predictions.

Astérix sure has Gaul *And a girlfriend in the latest comic installment*

Though France has produced many famous artists, intellectuals and statesmen who might serve as the iconic face of the nation, perhaps none is as universally recognizable – and beloved – as the cultural ambassador who is making a triumphant return to public attention: the cartoon Gaulish warrior Astérix. The first new Astérix book in five years finds the hero in a new situation – in love for the first time ever, with Latraviata, an enchanting Roman spy.

Astérix and Latraviata sold a record 5.6 million copies across Europe in a week. It's the 31st book featuring Gaul's most famous son since he and his sidekick Obélix appeared in 1959. During that run, the duo's exploits have sold more than 300 million books in 107 languages and dialects. Since the death of Astérix writer René Goscinny, artist Albert Uderzo has produced the series alone – around one book every five years. Meanwhile, newer products have also sprung up – animated movies, interactive video games and even a theme park. It all adds to an Astérix industry estimated at over $140 million a year.

But Astérix's popularity lies in the books and their deceptively clever, humorous and educational accounts of a Gaulish village's interaction with outside cultures and its resistance to the occupying Imperial Roman forces. Though the settings are ancient, the stories are punctuated with clever references to modern France.

Set in Roman-controlled Condatum, *Astérix and Latraviata* relies on those familiar elements, plus the romantic attraction, which predictably comes to naught. The end, though, finds Obélix's canine companion, Idéfix, proving some Gauls are as good at making love as they are at making war.

---

b Mark the sentences T (true) or F (false).

Astérix is the best-known representative of France.   T ✔   F ◯

1 Astérix has never been in love before.   T ◯   F ◯

2 The writer feels that the books are the key to Astérix's success, rather than other aspects of the industry.   T ◯   F ◯

3 There is no mention of recent events in the stories.   T ◯   F ◯

4 Astérix's love affair is successful.   T ◯   F ◯

c Find phrases in the article that mean the same or nearly the same as the following.

a person who represents their culture ..*iconic face of the nation*..

1 victorious comeback ....   4 does not have a successful outcome ....

2 two people ....   5 pet dog ....

3 adventures ....

d Now use a dictionary to check any words or phrases you are not sure about.

2 History and politics

Language summary: connectors

Use:		Form:		
We use connectors for the following reasons:				
• to indicate sequence, use *then, next, after that, in the end, a decade (day, week, month) later*, etc.		He opened the door.	**After that,**	he went out.
• to add a similar idea, use *also, in addition, furthermore*, etc.		They found it very difficult.	**In addition,**	they were exhausted.
• to give an opposing idea, use *however, but, although, in spite of*, etc.		This is a problem.	**However,**	I think we can solve it.
• to talk about cause and effect, use *therefore, as a result*, etc.		The taxi was very late.	**As a result,**	we missed our flight.

1 Language work

a Look back at the article *Glorious or ridiculous?* in your Student's Book (page 9). Look at how the following connectors are used and match them with the correct meaning. Be careful: there are two connectors for one of the meanings!

1 long before ⟶ **a)** to indicate sequence

2 eventually **b)** to add a similar idea

3 moreover **c)** to give an opposing idea

4 so **d)** to talk about cause and effect

5 while

b Rewrite the sentences to use *although* or *however*.

Although England had a revolution, its monarchy has lasted over a thousand years.

England had a revolution. However, its monarchy has lasted over a thousand years.

1 Although the human race has reached the moon, we seem unable to prevent wars.

....

2 Many people now use birth control. However, the population continues to grow.

....

3 Britain and Japan are considered advanced countries. However, they still have monarchies.

....

4 Although we have made huge technological progress, many of the world's people are still hungry.

....

2 **Skills work:** reading

Read these sentences and then put them in the correct order to form a paragraph.

.... This was largely because most buildings in Seattle were very solidly built with special protection against earthquakes.

.... There were then a number of aftershocks.

...1... Early in the year 2001, there was an earthquake in Seattle, U.S.

.... The residents of Seattle believe that eventually there could be a much bigger earthquake, which might even destroy their city.

.... Although it measured over 7 on the Richter scale, very few people were killed.

.... A great deal of damage was done, however, and people were extremely frightened since the initial earthquake lasted over 40 seconds.

3 **Skills work:** writing

Complete the text with a suitable connector from the box.

| although   as a result   eventually   ~~however~~   in addition to this   moreover |

In the 20th century, the world made huge advances, especially in science, medicine and technology.

However........................, there were still enormous problems. Much of the world's population was

still starving. **(1)** ...., environmental problems were increasing, largely

(2) .... of pollution caused by growth in industry. **(3)** ...., a

number of countries were living under constant threat of disaster and war. **(4)** .... we

have made great progress, it seems we are unable to live together in harmony and protect our environment.

(5) ...., if we are not careful, our planet may not survive.

3 Heroes and villains

1 Skills work: reading

Read this article about Michel Thomas and answer the questions.

Michel Thomas: a hero for our times

"I have lived many lives and had many identities"

Michel Thomas was born into a Jewish family in Łódź, Poland and was brought up largely by women before being captured by the Nazis, held in a concentration camp and forced into slave labor in a coal mine. While he was experiencing imprisonment, suffering and even torture, he began to develop his extraordinary psychological powers, which enabled him to resist pain and today make him one of the most successful and unusual language teachers in the world.

Thomas had spent several years in imprisonment when he escaped and joined the Secret Army of the Resistance. He eventually enlisted with the American forces and was fighting with them in Germany when Dachau was liberated. Thomas had lost his entire family during the war but, in spite of that, he organized a special Reconciliation Concert in Munich, to which both Germans and people from the Allied countries were invited. He felt it was important to bring the two sides together in an attempt to put the past behind them. Today, Thomas teaches languages to all kinds of people, from ghetto kids to movie stars, and has dramatic success even with those who have never managed to learn a language before. He has appeared on television several times, displaying his apparently magical gift for overcoming barriers and unlocking minds.

What makes Michel Thomas such a successful language teacher?
He has a gift for overcoming barriers and unlocking minds.
....

1 What did he do after he escaped from the concentration camp?

....

2 What was so special about the concert in Munich?

....

3 What does Thomas do now and why is he famous?

....

4 What is the meaning of the quote at the beginning of the text?

....

Language summary: past time clauses

Use:	Form:					
Use the past perfect to talk about an action that took place before another action (in the past simple), and link them with *when* or *after*. *After we **had eaten** lunch, we **relaxed** on the beach for an hour.*	The past perfect = subject + *had* + past participle					
	After	I	**had**	**spoken**	to her, I went to see the manager.	
	When	she		**finished**	the report, she passed it to me.	
Use the past simple to talk about an action happening while a longer one was in progress (in the past progressive), and link them with *when* or *while*. *I **was waiting** at the bus stop when the two cars **crashed**.*	The past progressive = subject + *was / were* + *-ing* form					
	While	I	**was**	**living**	in Mexico,	I met my future husband.
	When	they	**were**	**watching**	the game,	their house was burglarized.
	I		**was**	**living**	in Mexico	**when**	I met my future husband.
	They		**were**	**watching**	the game		their house was burglarized.

2 Language work

a Find three sentences with past time clauses in the article about Michel Thomas. Underline them.

b Join the two sentences in each pair, using *while*, *when* or *after*.

> **Language note**
> We use *when* to introduce either the shorter action or the longer one.
> We use *while* to introduce only the longer one.

He was captured by the Nazis. He was living in Poland.

He was captured by the Nazis while he was living in Poland. ....

1 He was suffering great pain. He began to develop special gifts.

....

2 He had escaped. He joined the Secret Army of the Resistance.

....

3 The war had finished. He organized a reconciliation concert.

....

3 Skills work: writing

a Think of a hero from your country. You could use the ideas from the discussion in your Student's Book (page 11). Make notes about the main events in this person's life:

Where and when born / Education / Events in early life / Achievements in later life / Main achievement

b Use your notes to write a short account of this person's life. Pay particular attention to your use of past time clauses.

.... (name) was born in .... in
....
He/She was brought up in ....

Unit 2 People and technology

1 Living with machines

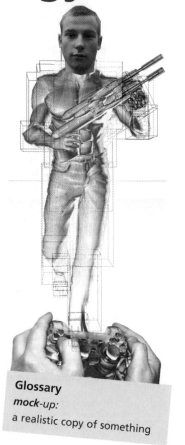

1 Skills work: reading

a Read this article and answer the questions in your own words.

> ### See yourself in cyberspace
>
> If you somehow can't identify with those anonymous computer game heroes and would love to put yourself, literally, into the picture instead, Digimask is great news. Using two photos of your face – a frontal shot and a profile – the technology first creates a 360° image of the head and then covers it with virtual skin and hair. Since the tool concentrates on skeletal structure and muscle placement, the result is an almost perfect likeness of the model, complete with lip and facial movement.
>
> To get your very own free-of-charge Digimask mock-up, all you have to do is register online at the software company's web site, provide a few details about your physical attributes – height, weight and so on – and send the two portraits by e-mail. Within the next ten minutes or so, you will receive your virtual clone by return mail and can employ it in any compatible game, using your own image as the hero. Digimask images may be used not only to personalize anonymous PC, PlayStation and X-Box games, but they can also be inserted into your e-mails, WAP messages and web site, and feature in videos and movies. And of course, your 3D picture will also come in handy on e-commerce sites, where it will allow you to try out those designer sunglasses before you buy them. In short, you can be a star in cyberspace.

Glossary
mock-up:
a realistic copy of something

1 What is Digimask? ....

2 How does it work? ....

3 What do you need to send to get a mock-up? ....

4 What are some different uses of Digimask? ....

b Look at these phrases from the article. Try to guess what they mean from the context or from similar phrases in your language. Write a short definition.

to put yourself, literally, into the picture   *to have your image on the screen*

1 an almost perfect likeness   ....

2 your physical attributes   ....

3 your virtual clone   ....

4 come in handy   ....

5 on e-commerce sites   ....

c Now use a dictionary to check your guesses.

2 Skills work: writing

a Make notes about the advantages and disadvantages of e-mail, under these headings.

Advantages	Disadvantages
You can contact people at any time.	People no longer write letters.

b Use your notes to write a paragraph comparing the advantages and disadvantages of e-mail. Try to use some of the connectors from unit 1.

3 Word work: multi-word verb meanings

a Match the multi-word verbs in the sentences with the definitions on the right.

1   The plane took off on time.
2   She took off her shoes.
3   They were brought up in Italy.
4   She brought up the issue of safety.
5   They set out the plans clearly.
6   We set out for New York in the morning.
7   She took over the driving.
8   Bloomingdale's has been taken over.
9   They came across some old coins.
10 He came across as very competent.

a) raise children
b) begin a trip / journey / course of action
c) take responsibility for
d) find by chance
e) buy (a company)
f) raise a topic
g) seem to be
h) explain / give details
i) leave the ground
j) remove

b Rewrite each sentence, using one of the multi-word verbs above.

The children were raised by their grandparents.
The children were brought up by their grandparents.

1 They left early for the islands.

....

2 He found some archeological remains by chance.

....

3 She took responsibility for the company when her father retired.

....

4 The plane left after a two-hour delay on the runway.

....

2 Genetic engineering

1 Word work: words about genetic engineering

a Look at these words and phrases from unit 2 lesson 2 in your Student's Book.
Write them in the correct column.

| ~~antibiotics~~ | bacteria | ~~cell~~ | clone | code | crops | designer babies | DNA | gene |
| inheritance | insecticides | junk food | pests | repel insects | rough draft | viruses |

Human genome project	GM foods
cell	antibiotics

b Use a dictionary to check the meaning and pronunciation of any words and phrases you aren't sure about.

2 Skills work: reading

a Read this questionnaire and check (✔) the most appropriate answer, according to **your** opinion.

	agree	not sure	disagree
1 Genetic engineering may help to eliminate disease.	◯	◯	◯
2 Drugs in the future may be designed for individuals.	◯	◯	◯
3 Some people will choose the exact characteristics of their babies.	◯	◯	◯
4 People will make clones of themselves.	◯	◯	◯
5 More and more people will choose organic foods, despite the cost.	◯	◯	◯
6 McDonald's will stop using GM foods.	◯	◯	◯
7 GM foods are more vulnerable to new viruses than organic foods.	◯	◯	◯
8 More and more farmers will return to traditional farming methods as they realize the dangers of GM crops.	◯	◯	◯

b Use your results from the questionnaire to write three or four predictions about genetic engineering.

....

....

....

....

....

Language summary: *whoever, whatever, whenever, however*

Use:	Form:
Use these words to express *it doesn't matter who / what / when / where.* *She speaks to me **whenever** she sees me.*	*wh-ever* + subject + verb: **Wherever** we go, we always find something of interest. I'll do **whatever** you ask. *wh-ever* + verb: **Whoever** wrote that book must be insane! **Whatever** happens in the election, there will be some changes.

3 Language work

a Match the beginnings of these sentences on the left with the endings on the right.

1 Wherever you lead,

2 Whatever mistakes you make,

3 Whenever I hear that song,

4 Whatever was said in the past

5 Whoever you loved before,

a) can be forgotten now.

b) I remember when we first met.

c) it's me you're with now.

d) I will follow.

e) I will always love you.

b Rewrite these sentences, using an appropriate *wh-ever* word.

It doesn't matter what you think about it, I don't agree with you.

Whatever you think about it, I don't agree with you. ....

1 It doesn't matter who told you that, they were wrong!

....

2 Every time I see him, my heart skips a beat.

....

3 It doesn't matter who you know, you won't get this job.

....

4 It doesn't matter where you look, you won't find it.

....

3 Technology dependence and risks

1 Language work: multi-word verbs and words that go with them

a In each group of nouns on the right, there is one that does not go with the multi-word verb on the left. Cross out the incorrect one in each case.

She switched on
the radio
her computer
the oven
~~the bathtub~~

1 I turned down
the candles
the volume
the music
my personal stereo

2 He came across
some pictures
a new word
the weather
an article about technophobia

3 She looked up
the phone number
the meaning
the dictionary
the past tense

4 I got over
the flu
my first boyfriend
the operation
my dinner

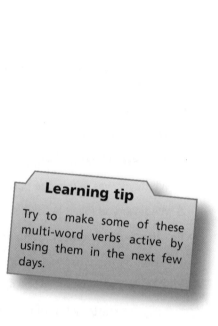

Learning tip

Try to make some of these multi-word verbs active by using them in the next few days.

b Now complete this spidergram with multi-word verbs that can take each of the nouns as objects. Use a dictionary to check if necessary.

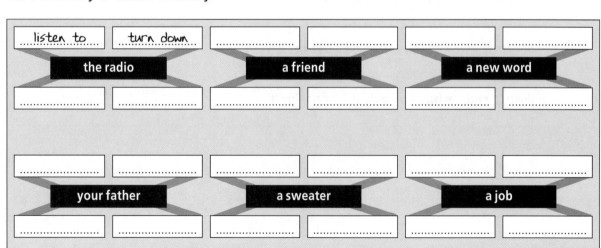

c Rewrite these sentences, using a pronoun as the object.

I turned down the radio. ...I turned it down....

1 She got over her terrible illness.

....

2 We ran into our old friends last week.

....

3 He tried out the computer before buying it.

....

4 I looked up the multi-word verb in the dictionary.

....

5 She takes after her parents.

....

> **Language note**
>
> Remember that some multi-word verbs are separable and others are not.
> *I switched on the lights.* or *I switched the lights on.* but *I came across an old photograph.*
> ✗ *I came an old photograph across.*
> If the object is a pronoun, it must go **between** the two parts of the separable verb but **after** both parts of the inseparable verb.
> Separable: *I switched them on.* ✗ *I switched on them.*
> Inseparable: *I came across it.* ✗ *I came it across.*

2 Pronunciation work: stress

Underline the stressed syllables in the sentences in exercise 1c.
I turned down the <u>rad</u>io.
I turned it <u>down</u>.

3 Skills work: writing

a Look at these phrases with multi-word verbs that describe activities in a typical day.
Check (✔) the first circle for the ones you do every day, or most days.

take off your clothes	◯ ◯	turn on the shower	◯ ◯
set off for work / college	◯ ◯	turn on the TV	◯ ◯
turn off the light	◯ ◯	get in the car	◯ ◯
get on the train / bus	◯ ◯	get up	◯ ◯
switch off the computer	◯ ◯	put on your clothes	◯ ◯
get down to work	◯ ◯	pick up a sandwich	◯ ◯

b Put the activities in the order in which you do them during the day (in the second circle).

c Write a paragraph about what you do every day, using the activities above and some others if you can. Try to use as many multi-word verbs as possible.

Every morning I get up, turn on the shower and wait for the water to heat up ...

Unit 3 Global versus local

1 The real thing

1 **Word work:** words and phrases about truth and falsehood

a Look at the words about truth and falsehood. Put them in the correct column and write the part of speech. Include one or two words that can go with them.
(Look back at *Fakes – a world of copycats* on page 24 of your Student's Book.)

> copy   counterfeit   fake   ~~genuine~~   illegal   legitimate   ~~pirate~~   real

Truth	Falsehood
genuine (adj) – genuine article, genuine goods	pirate (adj) – pirate cassettes, pirate software

b Use a dictionary to add other words and phrases, and to check meanings and pronunciation.

c Complete this text with words from the chart.

One of the things I most enjoyed about visiting Thailand was the shopping. We did most of it in the colorful street markets, which stayed open until after midnight. I was particularly struck by the number of c̲o̲u̲n̲t̲e̲r̲f̲e̲i̲t̲ goods on sale. These looked and smelled just like the **(1)** .... article but were clearly not the **(2)** .... thing. There were **(3)** .... perfumes, clothes and leather goods, all with the original brand name but somehow looking just slightly different. There were also **(4)** .... copies of videos and **(5)** .... cassettes. I found the whole thing very fascinating, but I have to admit that, like millions of others, I was not averse to picking up a really cheap pair of "Nikes" or some bargain "Ray-Bans".

2 Pronunciation work: /eɪ/, /eə/, /aɪ/

Say these words to yourself, then put them in the correct column according to the vowel sound (underlined in words of more than one syllable).

~~bikes~~ buyers ~~care~~ con<u>spi</u>re fair ~~fake~~ gains lo<u>ca</u>tion mail <u>Micro</u>soft	
<u>Ni</u>ke <u>pi</u>rate raid sales share trade world<u>wide</u>	

/eɪ/	/eə/	/aɪ/
fake	care	bikes

3 Skills work: writing

a Write about shopping in your country or in a country you have visited. Make notes next to these headings.

Description of the place ....

The kind of things on sale ....

What I liked / disliked ....

What I bought ....

b Now use your notes and the text about Thailand to complete this framework.

A lot of the shopping in .... takes place
in .... This / these ....
and .... There is a variety of things on sale,
including .... and ....
I found the whole thing .... and
and the .... I particularly liked the ....
.... but I was not so happy with the
...., which .... In the end
I bought ....

2 International and local food

1 Skills work: reading

a Look at the title and subtitle of this article. What do you understand by them? Do you think the article will be positive or negative about fast food?

b Read the article and check your prediction.

LET THEM EAT FRIES

AS BAGUETTES MAKE WAY FOR BIG MACS, A NEW BOOK SAYS FRANCE MAY BE LOSING THE GOOD FOOD FIGHT

When a group of sheep farmers led by José Bové trashed a McDonald's in Millau, France last year to protest about American taxes on Roquefort cheese, they struck a chord that resonated deeply throughout a country famous for its love of good food. As Bové rose to the rank of national hero, it became clear that his protest was about more than taxes; it was also about the French fight against *malbouffe*, or lousy food. McDonald's has become a symbol of harried modern life, where children clamor for *le Happy Meal* and the sacred midday repast may come prepackaged for convenience.

For many in France these trends signal not only a decline in food quality, but a decline in civilization as well.

The state of French cuisine in the era of fast food is the subject of *A goose in Toulouse* (Hyperion; 285 pages). Mort Rosenblum, a veteran Associated Press foreign correspondent, illustrates why every subject in France, from politics to business, is closely entwined with the national passion for food. In fact, Rosenblum argues, "Good food, with all that is behind it, is the defining metaphor of France." Even in revolutionary times, he

notes, one Frenchman reminded his fellow citizens, "Great events are fine ... but let's not forget lunch." Touring the country more than 200 years later, Rosenblum finds that the French still value lunch, but globalization and the Internet are changing the way they eat – and not always for the better. ...

Despite some positive developments, Rosenblum fears that his beloved French culture and cuisine may suffer in a world where commerce is king. One chef calls food the only reliable barometer for gauging the state of Frenchness. If he and Rosenblum are right, the forecast for France is stormy weather as the fast-food revolution continues its inexorable advance.

c Choose the correct answer.

		a)	b)
This article is:		a) a news item.	(b) a book review.)
1	McDonald's was attacked:	a) as a protest against the U.S.	b) to complain about taxation.
2	McDonald's represents:	a) all that is bad about fast food.	b) all that is bad about America.
3	Mort Rosenblum is also:	a) a translator.	b) a journalist.
4	In France, food is linked with:	a) everything.	b) politics and business.
5	Rosenblum has been touring France:	a) on vacation.	b) to investigate the state of French food.

d Find words in the article which mean the same or something similar to the following.

destroyed   trashed

1 sounded	....	5 meal	....
2 terrible	....	6 linked	....
3 stressful	....	7 measuring	....
4 demand	....	8 unstoppable	....

2 Skills work: writing

Look back at the two different frameworks for making notes in your Student's Book.
Choose one of them to make some notes on the advantages and disadvantages of fast food.

Advantages	Disadvantages
convenient	same wherever you go

Language summary: nouns in groups

Use:	Form:
To link two nouns together, when one belongs to or is related to the other: *history book, the boy's clothes*	noun + noun

car	window
table	leg

noun + 's + noun:

the girl's	books
the cat's	whiskers

3 Language work

Add nouns to each of these headwords to make appropriate combinations.

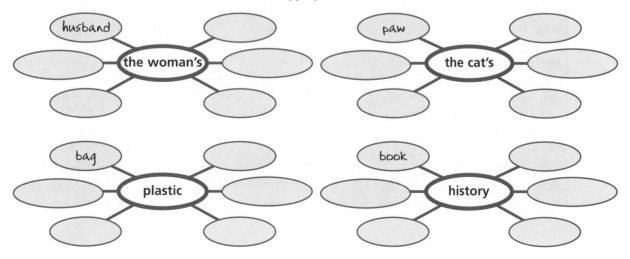

3 Hollywood versus Bollywood

1 Skills work: reading

a Read the article below and answer the questions.

How many movies are mentioned here? *Five movies are mentioned.* ....

1 Which movies are actually reviewed? ....

2 Write one of the movies next to each opinion, as expressed by the writer:

    a) mainly positive ....

    b) doesn't really give an opinion ....

    c) extremely negative ....

3 Does Jennifer Lopez play the bride in *The Wedding Planner?* ....

4 Give three reasons why George Sand scandalized Paris society:

    a) ....

    b) ....

    c) ....

Focus on movies

In case you hadn't realized, the vacation is just around the corner, which means kiddies' movies will be opening left, right and center in the next few weeks. This Friday we get *Spy Kids*, in which the son and daughter of two ace spies have to rescue their parents when they are kidnapped by a baddie, and *Rugrats in Paris*, in which Chuckie, Anjelica and the rest of the ankle-munchers go to ... Paris!

Please, if you can possibly avoid it, DON'T go see *The Wedding Planner*, the latest vehicle for sultry star Jennifer Lopez. Unfortunately, in this she shows none of the stunning sex appeal so upfront in *Out of Sight* with George Clooney. Here she is teamed with Matthew McConaughy, who plays the fiancé of the bride that Lopez is currently planning a wedding for. They fall in love of course, but how can she steal him from another woman, especially since the flowers are ordered, the dress has been made and the guests are all due to arrive?

It's the kind of sentimental nonsense that puts back women's causes by at least 20 years.

Juliette Binoche stars in *Les Enfants du Siècle* as famous writer George Sand. Sand absolutely stunned Paris society by dressing as a man and doggedly pursuing doomed composer Chopin, but the thing that got everybody really hot under the collar was her love affair with a younger poet, Alfred de Musset (Bénoit Magimel). The movie has stunning location work and the acting is superlative, but at two and a quarter hours it does slightly wear out its welcome.

b Look at these phrases from the article. Try to guess what they mean from the context or from similar phrases in your language. Write a short definition.

just around the corner   very soon ....

1 left, right and center   ....

2 sultry star   ....

3 sentimental nonsense   ....

4 doggedly pursuing   ....

5 hot under the collar   ....

c Now use a dictionary to check your guesses.

Language summary: indefinite pronouns

Use:	Form:		
Use indefinite pronouns in place of a noun when you do not know exactly who, exactly what or exactly where. *I know I've put my address book **somewhere**, but I can't find it.* Also use indefinite pronouns when the person, thing or place (subject or object) is not important. *I need **somebody** to help me with this luggage, please.*	some	one	**Someone** has broken the window. Are you going **somewhere**?
	any	body	I didn't tell **anybody**. She didn't do **anything**.
	every	thing	**Everyone** understands this. Why don't you tell me **everything**?
	no	where	**Nothing** happened last night. There's **nobody** at home.

2 Language work

Complete this e-mail with indefinite pronouns.

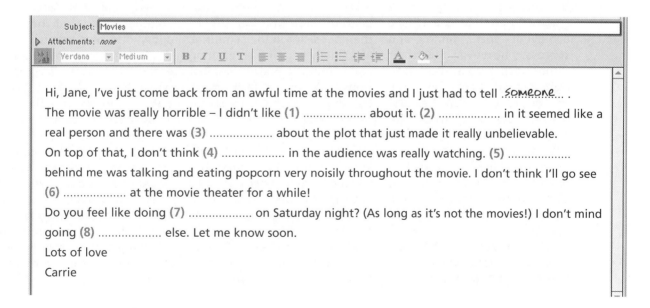

Subject: Movies

Attachments: *none*

Verdana   Medium   **B** *I* U̲ T

Hi, Jane, I've just come back from an awful time at the movies and I just had to tell .*someone*... .
The movie was really horrible – I didn't like **(1)** .... about it. **(2)** .... in it seemed like a real person and there was **(3)** .... about the plot that just made it really unbelievable.
On top of that, I don't think **(4)** .... in the audience was really watching. **(5)** ....
behind me was talking and eating popcorn very noisily throughout the movie. I don't think I'll go see
(6) .... at the movie theater for a while!
Do you feel like doing **(7)** .... on Saturday night? (As long as it's not the movies!) I don't mind
going **(8)** .... else. Let me know soon.
Lots of love
Carrie

Unit 4 Family, friends and colleagues

1 Brothers and sisters

1 Skills work: reading

a What do you know about the girls in the photograph? Write one question asking something you would like to know, then read the article to see if your question is answered.

THOSE AMAZING WILLIAMS SISTERS

The great tennis playing sisters, Venus and Serena Williams, shot to fame in the late 1990s. Both sisters won major titles before they hit 20, and were admired immediately for their extraordinary speed and athleticism as well as for the power and beauty of their game. They might never have achieved such fame and success, however, if their father, Richard, had not been right behind them every step of the way. When he first became aware of their rare childhood talent, he was determined that they would both become world-class players and the hours he put into their training and development have clearly had results.

Their parents already had three daughters when Venus was born in 1980, followed by Serena in 1981. Serena first caught the public eye in 1997 when she beat Monica Seles and Mary Pierce in Chicago. In the same year, Venus was the defeated finalist of the U.S. Open. She went on to become the Women's Champion at Wimbledon in 2000, after beating first Martina Hingis, then her sister in the semifinal, and finally winning an exciting and dramatic battle against Lindsay Davenport in the final. She then confirmed her status by winning the title again in 2001.

Both sisters are well-known for their somewhat unusual tennis wear and they appear to take delight in wearing colorful and sometimes revealing outfits on court. There has been a certain amount of criticism of their dress sense, particularly from more conservative members of the public, who feel that women tennis players should still be wearing demure white dresses. There have been rumors of rivalry between them and even allegations that some of their matches are rigged, and that Serena, the younger sister, will never be allowed to beat Venus.

Things came to a head in early 2001 at Indian Wells, when Venus suddenly pulled out of her semifinal match against Serena, complaining of a knee injury. There was a public outcry, which resulted in accusations of racism against the sisters. One of their great gifts, however, is their extraordinary resilience, and they both soon bounced back to delight the crowds once more with their incredible tennis.

b Read the article again and answer the questions.

How did the Williams sisters' father help them to become great?

He put a lot of time into their training and development.

1 Did Venus win the U.S. Open in 1997?

....

2 Who did she beat before playing Davenport in the Wimbledon final of 2000?

....

3 Why do some people object to the clothes Venus and Serena wear?

....

4 What accusations have been made against the sisters?

....

5 What happened at Indian Wells?

....

2 Word work: suffixes

a Make adjectives from the nouns and verbs
in the box and write them in the correct column.

~~respect~~ ~~access~~ passion thought
society knowledge response
delight consider beauty terror
compassion

> **Learning tip**
>
> Remember that we can add -ible, -able, -ate and -ful to nouns or verbs to form adjectives. Don't forget that there is sometimes a change in spelling: *sense-sensible, rely-reliable*; and sometimes not: *agree-agreeable*.
>
> Sometimes the base word changes completely: *eat-edible*. Check in a dictionary if you are not sure.

-able	-ible	-ate	-ful
respectable	accessible	....	....
....	....	....	....
....	....	....	....

b Write a sentence to describe each of these people. Try to use some of the adjectives above
or others with same suffixes.

1 your mother or father ....

2 your brother or sister ....

3 your boy/girlfriend ....

4 your best friend ....

5 your English teacher ....

2 All you need is love

1 Word work: phrases about love

a The following words can all go before or after the word *love*. Write them in the correct positions in the mind maps below.

~~platonic~~	~~letter~~	song	forbidden
affair	triangle	true	brotherly

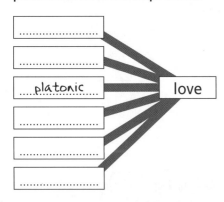

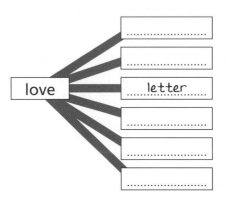

b Use a dictionary to check the meanings and pronunciation if necessary. Then add two more words to each mind map.

c Choose four phrases you want to remember and write a definition or an example.

love letter   a letter to a loved one, often largely about the relationship itself ....

1 ....

2 ....

3 ....

4 ....

Language summary: review of present tenses

Use:

Use the present simple for:
- habits and routines *We often **go** to the movies.*
- permanent situations *We **live** in New York.*
- facts *The sun **rises** in the east.*

Use the present progressive for:
- actions happening now or around now
  *She's **playing** baseball right now.*
- temporary actions and situations
  *He's **living** in Japan for a few months.*
- changes and developments
  *The Earth **is getting** hotter.*
- planned future events
  *We're **meeting** next week.*

Form:

Present simple = subject + verb (+ *s* or *es* for 3rd person singular)

I / you / we / they	**go**	to work by bus.
He / she	**goes**	

I / you / we / they	**don't go**	to work by bus.
He / she	**doesn't go**	

Do	I / you / we / they	**go** to work by bus?
Does	he / she	

Present progressive = subject + *is* / *are* + *-ing* form.

I / you / we / they	**are (n't)**	**feeling** very well.
He / she	**is (n't)**	

24

2 Language work

Dear Sam,

I'm writing to let you know how everything's going here. At the moment I'm sitting in my new study, which faces the park. I don't normally work here in the mornings – I usually go to the office downtown, but my boss is away right now so I'm spending a little more time at home!

Mads is enjoying her new job and is getting really good on the computer. The kids are starting at their new school next week. At the moment they are all painting their rooms, which is keeping them nice and quiet.

This weekend we're having a barbecue with some neighbors. They live in a beautiful house not far away with a huge back yard – they even have a swimming pool! It might be too cold to swim this time but we're taking our swimming suits just in case.

We're all missing you and we talk about you often.

Looking forward to hearing from you,

Present simple	Present progressive
habits and routines	happening now or around now ....
....	....
permanent situations	temporary actions or situations ....
....	....
facts	changes and developments ....
....	....
	planned future actions ....
	....

3 Working relations

1 Word work: words and phrases about communication

Look at these words and phrases about communication from your Student's Book. When you are trying to communicate effectively, do these phrases represent positive, negative or neutral ideas? Write them in the table.

~~non-verbal communication~~	jargon	distrust
let your mind wander		keep an open mind
maintain eye contact		scratch your head
facial expressions	gesture	posture
yawn	frown	glare	nod your head

Positive	Negative	Neutral
....	....	non-verbal communication
....	....	....
....	....	....
	....	....
	....	
	....	
	....	

2 Skills work: writing

a Write two or three points under the headings below, using the ideas in your Student's Book to help you.

Communication at work	Communication with family / friends
more use of specialized language	more physical

b Use your notes to help you write a paragraph about the differences between communication at work and communication with family and friends. Use this framework to help you.

> There are many differences between the way most people communicate in different situations. At work, people are generally much more ....
> ....
> and .... With family and friends, however, most people communicate.................................. . In my family ....

Language summary: verbs that do not take the progressive

Use:

We do not usually use the progressive form with verbs that:

- talk about states that are not usually continuing processes, e.g. *like, want, believe, know*
  *I **believe** you **want** to see me? **Do** you **know** what the time is?*

- talk about actions that are instantaneous, e.g. *notice, smell, throw, hit*
  ***Did** you **notice** Marta at the concert? **Do** you **smell** something strange here?*

3 Language work

a Look at these pairs of sentences. In each pair, choose the definition that best illustrates the meaning of the verb.

1 She thinks it's very beautiful.   ....b...

   She believes it's very beautiful.
   ....

2 He's thinking about his new job.   ....

   ....

   > a) to reflect on something
   > b) to believe / have an opinion

3 This tea tastes delicious..   ....

   ....

4 He's tasting the wine.   ....

   ....

   > a) to be
   > b) to try something

5 I'm seeing my mother tomorrow.   ....

   ....

6 I see what you mean.   ....

   ....

   > a) to understand
   > b) to meet

7 This fabric feels real soft.   ....

   ....

8 She was feeling dizzy.   ....

   ....

   > a) to have a (physical or emotional) sensation
   > b) to be

b Rewrite each sentence in a different way, to show the meaning of the verb.

Unit 5 The best of the past

1 The history of pop culture

1 **Skills work:** reading

a Look at the photo. Do you know this person? Check (✔) six words that you think will be in the article about him.

culture ◯ lyrics ◯

folk ◯ poet ◯

impenetrable ◯ tour ◯

inspiration ◯ writer ◯

lifestyle ◯

b Read the article quickly and check your answers.

In 2001 Bob Dylan turned 60. He also won an Oscar for the song *Things have changed* from the movie *The Wonder Boys*, starring Michael Douglas. This is an extract from an article about him, written in March 2001.

Hanif Kureishi,
WRITER

In the Sixties and Seventies, the people who proved themselves as songwriting geniuses were Bob Dylan, and Lennon and McCartney. It's rare to find people who can continue to write that quality of music. Dylan has remained creatively alive, maybe because he's allied himself to folk and blues, like the Stones, and manages to write good lyrics, sing and perform well. But Dylan's not necessarily an entertainer, he's a poet and the moody poet stuff is still his sign. He's dark and black but does it without sounding self-pitying.

P. J. Harvey,
SINGER

I am an enormous Bob Dylan fan. I once said *Desire* was my favorite album, but it changes all the time. He has been a big influence on my work. I grew up on a diet of Dylan – my mom was a big fan – and now when I'm feeling lost or lacking in inspiration I listen to him. It's not just his wonderful lyrics, it's the mixture of everything: the words, the music, and his voice. If you have a voice without soul, it doesn't move you. All the ingredients have to work together. But Dylan is beyond music and lyrics, he has something else. It's that indefinable something else that makes him special.

John Peel,
BROADCASTER

I have mixed feelings about Dylan. I know he does this punishing tour schedule but I am always outraged at his refusal to communicate with the people who pay for him to be there. He did some great experimentation with different voices in the Seventies and Eighties and I think his greatest legacy is that he made it possible for people who can't sing to make records. He opened the door to impenetrable lyrics and songs that don't contain their title. He was the first person to do that. He did kick open doors that needed opening and have remained open. We have to be enormously grateful to him for making songs that record companies did not appreciate but became commercially successful and thus in a sense led the way to punk.

c   Read the article again and answer the questions.

What exactly does Bob Dylan do, according to the writers?

He's a songwriter, a singer and a poet.

1 Which of these commentaries would you say is the odd one out? Explain why.

....

2 Name three things that both Hanif Kureishi and P. J. Harvey say they like about Dylan.

....

3 What do you think is the main thing John Peel does not like about Dylan?

....

4 Which of the writers:

a) says that Dylan's songs are hard to understand? ....

b) talks about Dylan the poet? ....

c) talks about the emotional quality of his voice? ....

d   Look at these phrases from the article. Try to guess what they mean from the context or from similar phrases in your language. Write a short definition.

I grew up on a diet of Bob Dylan ....*I listened to a lot of Bob Dylan.*........................

1 lacking in inspiration ....

2 this punishing tour schedule ....

3 outraged ....

4 his greatest legacy ....

5 impenetrable lyrics ....

e   Now use a dictionary to check your definitions.

2   **Word work:** words and phrases about music
    Complete this spidergram with words and phrases about music.
    Use your previous knowledge and a dictionary to help you.

instruments		**types**
violin		blues
....	**music**	....
....		....
words about songs		**musicians**
lyrics		guitarist
....		....
....		....

2 Revolutionaries past and present

Language summary: the past

Use:	Form:
Use the past simple: • to describe a setting in the past • to describe an action or event in the past	Examples: *It **was** a stormy night.* *Lightning **struck** the house.*
Use the past progressive: • to describe a setting in the past • to talk about an action in progress in the past when another one started	 *The sun **was setting**.* *They **were sleeping** when the fire started.*
Use *there was / were* to describe a setting in the past	***There was** no one on the streets.*
Use the past perfect to talk about one action that took place before another action in the past	*They **had gone** to bed three hours before the fire started.*
Use *must, may, might* or *couldn't* + present perfect to make deductions about the past • with *must* the speaker is 99% sure it happened • with *couldn't* the speaker is 99% sure it **didn't** happen • with *may / might* the speaker thinks it is possible that it happened	*It **must have rained** as all the streets are wet.* *It **must** have happened.* *It **couldn't** have happened.* *It **may / might** have happened.*

1 Language work

a Complete this article about riots in Cincinnati with the past simple, past progressive or past perfect of the verb given in parentheses.

Revolution on the streets?

Last night hundreds of police officers were patrolling (patrol) Cincinnati's empty streets as they (1) .... (struggle) to bring an end to some of America's worst urban rioting for a generation.

The authorities (2) .... (declare) a state of emergency yesterday and (3) .... (impose) a citywide curfew after two nights of full-scale rioting following a police shooting of an unarmed black suspect.

America's latest urban crisis (4) .... (begin) after a white Cincinnati police officer (5) .... (shoot) and (6) .... (kill) 19-year-old Timothy Thomas last Saturday. The police (7) .... (look for) him because he (8) .... (fail) to appear in court on misdemeanor and traffic charges. It was the 15th time the Cincinnati police (9) .... (shoot) and (10) .... (kill) a black man since 1995, and the fourth incident since November.

Local black leaders (11) .... (say) they had warned the police repeatedly that their patience (12) .... (wear) thin. "People will rebel if they don't see themselves making progress," (13) .... (say) the Rev. Fred Shuttlesworth, a 79-year-old local civil rights activist who (14) .... (march) with Martin Luther King in the 1960s. "The riots that are happening are the result of Cincinnati not responding and not changing enough."

b Complete the deductions based on this text, using *must, may, might* or *couldn't* + present perfect.

In late May 2001 the peace of the streets of Oldham, a town in north-west England, was shattered by riots that lasted two days. No one knows the true cause of the riots, but it seems to have been racial tension between different communities. It's possible that the murder of an elderly white man some time before was the underlying cause. Police sources suggest that the real cause was outsiders coming into the town to provoke problems between the races, although leaders of the Asian community feel that the situation definitely worsened because of the police response.

Whatever the cause of the riots, only a few days later, in the general election, the candidate for the British National Party (an extreme right-wing party with racist tendencies) received more votes than anyone from that party in the past. The party clearly benefited from the racial tension of the previous few weeks, indicating that the people of Oldham were clearly unhappy about the situation in their town.

The cause of the riot *might have been racial tension.* ....

1 The underlying cause ....

2 The police think outsiders ....

3 Asian community leaders believe ....

4 The British National Party ....

5 The people of Oldham ....

2 **Word work:** words and phrases about riots

a Look at these phrases from the article about Cincinnati. Try to guess what they mean from the context or from similar phrases in your language. Write a short definition.

to bring an end to   *to stop* ....

1 citywide   ....

2 an unarmed suspect   ....

3 a misdemeanor   ....

4 to wear thin   ....

5 a civil rights activist   ....

b Now use a dictionary to check your guesses.

3 Viewpoint

1 Skills work: reading

a Read this article and find words or phrases to label the picture.

Frank Lloyd Wright

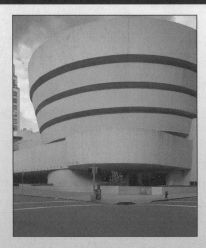

Frank Lloyd Wright is arguably the twentieth century's greatest architect. His career spanned seventy years, from the 1880s to the 1950s. He was a prolific worker and designed 1,141 buildings, of which 532 were built and 409 still stand today. Lloyd Wright designed a wide range of buildings, from public buildings to houses. These buildings were constructed in different states throughout America and a few were also constructed in Japan, England and Canada. Twenty of these buildings are currently open to the public, for example the Guggenheim Museum in New York.

Lloyd Wright believed that people are affected by the environments in which they live. He was greatly influenced by the power of nature and this was reflected in his designs and his choice of building materials. He manipulated brick, stucco, wood, plaster, stone, concrete and copper in a way that had never been done before. Lloyd Wright did not design only the outside of buildings; he also designed their insides. He believed that the exterior and interior of buildings should be similar, and should move naturally from each other.

Well-known styles of houses designed by Lloyd Wright are the prairie style of the early 1900s and the Usonian style from the mid 30s until Lloyd Wright's death. The prairie house was a long, low building with an emphasis on horizontal lines. The Usonian style developed from the prairie style and was designed specifically as low-income housing. Other examples of Lloyd Wright's style are shingle-style and Chicago School.

b Mark the sentences (T) true or (F) false? Put a check (✔) in the right circle.

It is still possible to see examples of Lloyd Wright's work.   T ✔   F ◯

1 There are 1,141 Lloyd Wright buildings in America.   T ◯   F ◯

2 Most of Lloyd Wright's buildings were constructed in Europe.   T ◯   F ◯

3 Lloyd Wright used a lot of natural materials in his designs.   T ◯   F ◯

4 Lloyd Wright designed the interior of buildings.   T ◯   F ◯

5 Lloyd Wright made houses for the very poor to live in.   T ◯   F ◯

c Look at these figures from the text. What is their significance?

1880s *when Frank Lloyd Wright started his career* ....

1 early 1900s ....

2 532 ....

3 1950s ....

4 mid 30s ....

5 1,141 ....

6 20 ....

2 Word work: recording vocabulary

a Match these words from the article with their definitions. Use the context to help you.

1 arguably	**a)** extremely productive
2 spanned	**b)** open to discussion (but is probably true)
3 prolific	**c)** controlled in a skillful way
4 constructed	**d)** covered
5 manipulated	**e)** built
6 exterior	**f)** the outside

b Record the words and phrases from exercise 2a in your notebook. If you like, you can use a combination of recording methods for some of the words and phrases.

3 Skills work: writing

Read the text below and look carefully at each line. Some of the lines are correct and some have a mistake. Check (✔) the correct lines and correct the mistakes.

> **Learning tip**
>
> On page 47 of your Student's Book, you looked at different ways of recording vocabulary: a mind map, writing words in context, and making lists with translations. Sometimes you might combine two of these to really help you remember. You can also write a definition and you can include information about the pronunciation (by underlining the word stress) and the part of speech (in parentheses):
>
> sig<u>ni</u>ficance (n) – importance or meaning (What is the significance of these dates?)

Frank Lloyd Wright was a well-known ʌmerican architect	*American* ....
1 who died in the 1950s. For his career he designed	....
2 a number of buildings, of which 409 are still standing.	....
3 Most of his buildings are constructed in the United States	....
4 but there are a few in Japen, England and Canada.	....
5 Although Lloyd Wright died almost since 50 years, his	....
6 work is still influential.	....

33

Unit 6 Our century

1 Future shock

1 Skills work: reading

a Read this book review and answer the questions.

What kind of novel is *The Handmaid's Tale?*

It is a science fiction novel.

1 What happens to fertile women in the novel?

....

2 Why does this happen to them?

....

3 What happens to people who protest?

....

4 What is the mood of the novel like?

....

5 What happens to Offred in the end?

....

b Find these words in the article and write the noun that follows each one.

chilling   vision   frightening.............

1 gripping   ....

2 fertile   ....

3 childbearing ....

4 high-ranking ....

5 clandestine   ....

6 pervades   ....

7 bleak   ....

c Now try to guess what the words mean and write a synonym or a short definition of each.

Many books have been written about a particular vision of the future, though perhaps not all of these would be classed as science fiction. One of the most chilling visions is that described by Margaret Atwood in *The Handmaid's Tale.*

In this very scary but gripping novel, the Canadian feminist portrays a world in which fertile women of childbearing age – of whom few remain – are controlled by the state and are "owned" by powerful men for the purposes of breeding and sexual pleasure. Dissenters are either hanged or left to die a slow death by radiation sickness.

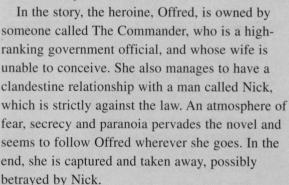

In the story, the heroine, Offred, is owned by someone called The Commander, who is a high-ranking government official, and whose wife is unable to conceive. She also manages to have a clandestine relationship with a man called Nick, which is strictly against the law. An atmosphere of fear, secrecy and paranoia pervades the novel and seems to follow Offred wherever she goes. In the end, she is captured and taken away, possibly betrayed by Nick.

This is a book that is very hard to put down, and the somewhat bleak vision of the future is counterbalanced by the exciting plot and the wit and humanity with which the author writes.

Glossary
dissenter: someone who refuses to accept official policy or decisions

2 Word work 1: synonyms and near-synonyms

a All these verbs and phrases are in Units 1–5 of this book. Try to remember their meaning without looking back and match them with the synonyms (or near-synonyms) on the right.

1 to get over		a)	to demand
2 to lack		b)	to measure
3 to come across		c)	to recover
4 to trash		d)	to withdraw
5 to gauge		e)	not to have
6 to clamor for		f)	to destroy
7 to be right behind someone		g)	to find by chance
8 to pull out of		h)	to support
9 to propel		i)	to move, drive

b Choose five of these verbs or phrases (the ones you had most difficulty remembering) and write a sentence to illustrate their meaning.

1 ....

2 ....

3 ....

4 ....

5 ....

3 Word work 2: guessing meaning from context

a Read this text and try to guess what the underlined words mean. Write your guesses below.

It was a **(1)** <u>sweltering</u> day and I was so hot I **(2)** <u>divested</u> <u>myself</u> first <u>of</u> my jacket then of my shirt. I was **(3)** <u>ambling</u> along through the **(4)** <u>meadow</u> of flowers when suddenly I sensed something behind me. I **(5)** <u>spun around</u> to see an **(6)** <u>irate</u>-looking farmer behind me. "You're trespassing on my land," he **(7)** <u>bellowed</u>, " and, if you must do that, I'd appreciate if you would do it in decent **(8)** <u>attire</u>."

> **Learning tip**
>
> Do you remember the strategies for guessing meaning from context, e.g. using the grammar of the word, looking at words around it? If not, go back to page 51 of your Student's Book and read the Learning tip again.

1 <u>very hot</u>	4	7 ....
2	5	8 ....
3	5	

b Now check your guesses in a dictionary and correct them if necessary.

2 The best intentions

1 Word work: words about plans and decisions

a Complete this table with nouns and adjectives based on these verbs.
There may be more than one possibility in some cases.

Verb	Noun	Adjective
intend	intention	....
determine	....	....
decide	....	....
resolve	....	....
plan	....	....
expect	....	....

b Use a dictionary to check the word stress and mark it by underlining the stressed syllable.

Language summary: future simple, *be going to*, future perfect

Use:	Form:
Use the future simple to talk about a decision made at the time of speaking. *Hold on. I'll give you a lift to the station.*	Future simple: subject + *will / won't* + verb <table><tr><td>I / you / we they</td><td>will</td><td rowspan="2">come tonight.</td></tr><tr><td>He / she</td><td>won't</td></tr></table>
Use *be going to* to talk about definite plans and decisions made before the time of speaking. *He's going to study medicine and become a doctor.*	*be going to*: subject + *to be* + *going to* + verb <table><tr><td>I / you / we / they</td><td>are (n't)</td><td rowspan="2">going to study for another year.</td></tr><tr><td>He / she</td><td>is (n't)</td></tr></table>
Use the future perfect to talk about an action that will be completed by a particular time in the future. *Next month we'll have been in this apartment for ten years.*	Future perfect: subject + *will / won't* + *have* + past participle <table><tr><td>I / you / we / they</td><td>will</td><td rowspan="2">have</td><td rowspan="2">finished by then.</td></tr><tr><td>He / she</td><td>won't</td></tr></table>

2 Language work

a Correct the mistakes of future forms in this letter.

> Dear Susie,
>
> I thought I'd write and let you know about my ideas for my vacation. First, I going to fly to Bangkok, where I to meet my friend Charlie. She's working in Malaysia, and by next month, she has been there for two years, so I'm sure she could use a break. I think we then catching another plane to an island in the southern part of Thailand, where we spend two weeks just lying on the beach. I think we have gotten a pretty good suntan by the end of our stay. After that, we are go to fly to Chiang Mai, where we do some trekking in the hills. Unfortunately, I have to fly home to Washington at the end of April, since I'm going try to find a new job in May.
> I see you then.
>
> > With love,
> >
> > > Ally

b Read these questions and check (✔) the best answer for you.

	definitely	possibly	definitely not
1 I'm going to find a (new) job in the next 12 months.	○	○	○
2 I think I'll try to lose some weight soon.	○	○	○
3 I'm going to save a lot more money.	○	○	○
4 Ten years from now I will have been married at least three times.	○	○	○
5 I will have had several jobs by then.	○	○	○
6 I think I'll travel and see some of the world.	○	○	○

3 Skills work: writing

Think of three or four resolutions that you'd like to make about your life in the future. (Look at page 53 of your Student's Book, exercise 5.) Use your resolutions and your answers to the questionnaire above to help you write a summary of your plans / how you see your life developing in the next five to ten years. Use this framework to help you.

> In the next year ....
>
> By this time next year, I think ....
>
> In the next four or five years ....
>
> By the time I am .... I hope ....
>
> and in about ten years, I ....

3 Biosphere

1 Skills work: reading

a Read this article quickly. Write an explanation of "reality TV".

....

The growth of reality TV

One of the great media sensations in the year 2000 was the massive growth and popularity of the so-called "reality TV" program. Ordinary individuals were chosen to be put in a particular situation and then scrutinized by the camera and the public, who watched their every move and examined their reactions.

Television in the United States offered many variations on this theme. One successful reality show was *Big Brother*, in which a group of strangers lived together in a house, watched 24 hours a day by TV cameras. No one was allowed to leave the house and they had to do a variety of challenging tasks as a team. Each week the group voted for two contestants to leave the show until there was one clear winner.

Another successful reality show was *Temptation Island*. Couples were separated from one another for two weeks. Their commitment to each other was tested as they went on blind dates with contestants of the opposite sex. However, the most successful reality show in the U.S. was *Survivor,* where only the toughest made it to the end of the show.

In *Survivor* sixteen people were given forty-two days to survive in the Outback in Australia. There could only be one winner. The sixteen participants, of a range of ages and occupations, were dropped off by plane in what seemed like the middle of nowhere. They had five minutes to take whatever they could from a crate of supplies. Divided into two

teams, or "tribes" as they were called, they had to complete a five-mile hike to their campsites. The campsites were four miles apart from each other, on opposite sides of a river. Once they arrived, the participants faced a series of real challenges and one by one they were eliminated. The sole survivor received the ultimate prize – $1,000,000!

Glossary

blind date: an arrangement to go out with someone you have never met before.

b Now read the article again and answer the questions.

1 Who decided which contestants should leave the show on *Big Brother*?

....

2 How is commitment tested in *Temptation Island*?

....

3 How many people were in each tribe in *Survivor*?

....

4 What is the final aim of *Survivor*?

....

c Find these words in the text. Then find another word in the text that means the same, or nearly the same, as each word.

individuals .....people...........................

1 program .... 4 survive ....

2 scrutinized .... 5 a series of ....

3 contestant ....

2 Word work: words about character

a The following are all words that can be used to describe character. Make sure you know the exact meanings and then check (✔) the ones you think would be an advantage in *Survivor*.

tough ○	practical ○	unrealistic ○	brave ○
uninventive ○	weak ○	cowardly ○	creative ○
self-sufficient ○	bad-tempered ○	dependent ○	stubborn ○
cooperative ○	adaptable ○	unimaginative ○	inflexible ○

b Write a sentence or two saying why you think you would or would not be a suitable candidate for *Survivor*. Try to use some of the adjectives above.

....

....

....

3 Language work: review of future forms

Look at these sentences containing future forms. Match a sentence on the left with one on the right, with the same future form.

1 The plane leaves at 7:00.

2 I can't decide ... OK, I'll get the red one.

3 This time next week, I'll be lying on a beach.

4 Be careful! It's going to break.

5 By tonight he'll have taken all his exams.

6 Don't worry. I'll help you.

7 She's going to study Italian.

8 I'm meeting her after work.

9 I'll call you when I arrive.

10 I know he won't come.

a) Look at those clouds. It's going to rain.

b) She'll be arriving in two hours' time.

c) No, I won't write ... I'll call you.

d) They're going to visit Chiang Mai.

e) We'll write as soon as we can.

f) The class begins next week.

g) I'm sure that movie will be good.

h) They're seeing each other next week.

i) Call at 8.00. I'll have eaten dinner by then.

j) I'll carry it if you like.

Unit 7 The world of sport

1 Your view

1 Word work: sports injuries

a Match the part of the body with the injury. There may be more than one possibility.

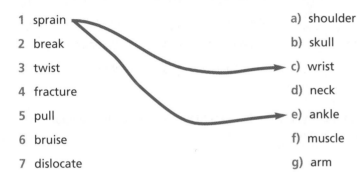

1 sprain   a) shoulder
2 break   b) skull
3 twist   c) wrist
4 fracture   d) neck
5 pull   e) ankle
6 bruise   f) muscle
7 dislocate   g) arm

> **Learning tip**
>
> Always try to notice the context that new words and phrases appear in. For example, in exercise 1a, only one verb can go with *muscle*. Which one?

b Make sentences with five of the combinations from exercise 1a.

I broke my arm while I was playing football.

1 ....
2 ....
3 ....
4 ....
5 ....

2 Skills work: reading

a Look at the photograph and select a caption.

1 A good day at work
2 Diving towards heaven?
3 A winter's day

b Read the article quickly and check your prediction.

Ordinary and extreme sports

Can you tell the difference between ordinary sports and extreme sports? What makes a sport "extreme" is taking it to the absolute limits. We've all heard of bungee jumping, skydiving, rock climbing, freestyle snowboarding. What they all have in common is that they challenge the participants and take them close to the edge.

But these are nothing compared to BASE jumping. BASE stands for Building, Antenna, Span (bridges) and Earth (cliffs) and is a very intense form of skydiving. Whereas skydivers use large parachutes to jump out a plane at approximately 12,000 feet, BASE jumpers leap off buildings, antennas, bridges or cliffs as low as 100 feet high, with only a small parachute on their backs.

BASE jumpers have been known to seek out well-known landmarks to jump off. The Eiffel Tower, Table Mountain, the Golden Gate Bridge, the Empire State Building, the Statue of Liberty, the Leaning Tower of Pisa … all are irresistible to jumpers in pursuit of the ultimate experience.

The "sport" is illegal in many countries so jumps often have to take place in the middle of the night. Deaths sometimes happen and injuries occur frequently. Nevertheless, extreme sporters are not deterred by the danger. The greater the risk, the bigger the thrill and the better the exhilaration.

c Read the article again and answer the questions.

Why do people choose to do extreme sports?

<u>Because they are looking for challenge and adventure.</u>

1 Why is rock climbing an extreme sport?

....

2 What is the basic difference between skydiving and BASE jumping?

....

3 Which of the BASE elements does the Statue of Liberty fall under?

....

4 According to the article, what makes BASE jumping dangerous?

....

d Find phrases in the article that mean the same or nearly the same as the following.

final level <u>absolute limits</u>

1 on the brink of ....   4 looking for ....

2 search for ....   5 happen ....

3 famous ....

2 The business view

<table>
<tr><td colspan="2">Language summary: review and extension of relative clauses</td></tr>
<tr><td>Use:</td><td>Form:</td></tr>
<tr>
<td>

Use relative pronouns (*that, who, which*) to join two clauses.

*There's the house **that** is being knocked down.*

When the relative pronoun is the object of the relative clause, it can be omitted.

The man you saw going into my house is an old friend.

When there is a preposition in the relative clause, this is often put at the end of the clause.

*That's the school **(that)** the children will be going to.*

</td>
<td>

Main clause + (relative pronoun) + relative clause
With a subject relative pronoun:

| Auto racing is a sport | which / that | involves some danger. |

With an object relative pronoun:

| Auto racing is a sport | (which) / (that) | many people enjoy. |

| Auto racing is a career | (which) / (that) | many boys aspire **to**. |

</td>
</tr>
</table>

1 Language work

a **Join the two ideas, using a relative clause. Omit the relative pronoun wherever possible.**
Red Marauder is a horse. It won the Grand National.

Red Marauder is a horse that won the Grand National.

1 Horse racing is a sport. It can be very dangerous.

....

2 That is the jockey. I saw him in last year's race.

....

3 Rivaldo is a soccer player. He comes from Brazil.

....

4 Consistency is an important quality. Many athletes are admired for this quality.

....

5 Tennis is a sport. It makes great demands on players.

....

6 The Baltimore Ravens are a soccer team. Randall Cunningham plays for this team.

....

b Now make up your own sentences, including a relative clause, about the following.

1 Pele ....

2 the Chicago Bears ....

3 the Williams sisters ....

4 women's soccer ....

2 Word work: sports equipment and places

a Complete the table with the equipment usaed in each sport and places where the sports are played.

Sport	Equipment	Place
soccer	ball, goals	field / stadium
baseball	....	....
basketball	....	....
tennis	....	....
boxing	....	....
skiing	....	....
running	....	....
surfing	....	....

b Write a sentence about three sports from the table, using a relative clause.
(Note that we don't use *play* with all of these sports; try *take place*.)

Soccer is a sport that is played on a field, with a ball and goals. ....

1 ....

2 ....

3 ....

3 Skills work: writing

Now think of a sport you know well and write a paragraph describing it. Make notes, to give you some ideas. Start with the sentence you wrote about the sport in exercise 2b, or a similar sentence.

Name of sport: ....

Equipment needed: ....

Place where it's played: ....

Number of players: ....

Object of the game: ....

Scoring system: ....

Qualities needed to play it: ....

Why people enjoy watching it: ....

Your feelings about it: ....

3 The career view

1 Skills work: reading

a Read the article quickly. What is the main aspect of drug taking that the ITF wants to highlight?

....

ITF campaigns to keep tennis drug-free

The International Tennis Federation, with the help of such stars as Russia's Anna Kournikova, launched a campaign Tuesday to keep junior tennis players drug-free.

The campaign, co-financed by the European Union, will highlight some of the physical side effects of steroid abuse, including cancer, cardiovascular disease, liver and kidney disease and high blood pressure.

"This is an important campaign. There are many pressures to win when you start out on the junior circuit," Kournikova said at a news conference in Den Bosch, the Netherlands, where the Davis Cup match between Germany and the Netherlands will be played beginning Friday. "The dangers of taking drugs may not be known to young people, and I hope that the ITF campaign will help change that. Drugs do not have a place in sports."

Men's No. 2 Gustavo Kuerten agreed. "I hope that the ITF campaign will ensure that aspiring players are aware of the dangers and consequences of taking performance-enhancing drugs," Kuerten said.

Tennis has had few documented cases of drug abuse. ITF President Francesco Ricci Bitti wants to keep it that way. "The virtual absence of drugs at the professional level sets a good example for the junior player, but sometimes something stronger, like this campaign, is needed to make the point."

---

b Mark the sentences T (true) or F (false).

The campaign is entirely financed by the ITF.   T ◯   F ☑

1 Anna Kournikova is leading the campaign.   T ◯   F ◯

2 Some players take drugs to help them win.   T ◯   F ◯

3 The campaign is aimed at younger players.   T ◯   F ◯

4 Anna Kournikova is playing in the Davis Cup in Den Bosch.   T ◯   F ◯

5 Drug abuse has been a major problem in tennis.   T ◯   F ◯

c Complete these expressions from the article, using one of the words from the box.
Try to do this from memory first, then check in the article.

point   absence   level   enhancing   junior   pressure   ~~launch~~   side

1 to ......*launch*...... a campaign   5 performance- .... drugs

2 physical .... effects   6 virtual ....

3 high blood ....   7 at the professional ....

4 on the .... circuit   8 to make the ....

Language summary: more relative clauses and modifying phrases

Use:	Form:
Use a defining relative clause to define or specify who or what we are talking about. *The Mets are one of the teams **that are based in New York.***	Defining relative clause: main clause + (relative pronoun) + relative clause Juan Pablo Montoya is the only Formula 1 driver **who comes from Colombia.**
Use a non-defining relative clause to add information about a person or thing. This is separated from the main clause by commas and the sentence would still make sense if the clause were omitted. *The players, **who were really tired,** decided to go home.*	Non-defining relative clause: main clause, + relative pronoun + relative clause Mark attributes his success to his parents, **who were right behind him all the way.**
It is not always necessary to use a relative clause to specify what we are talking about. We use modifying phrases as another way of doing this. *The Mets are one of the teams **living in / based in / from New York.***	Modifying phrases <ul><li>*-ing* form: Can you see the player **wearing the blue shorts?**</li><li>past participle: He's the one **chosen for the first team.**</li><li>prepositional phrase: How much is the racket **in the window?**</li></ul>

---

2 Language work

Rewrite these sentences using one of the ways in the Language summary. Omit the relative clause where it is non-defining and the relative pronoun wherever possible. Use a modifying phrase if you can.

My cousin, who is a dentist, lives in Detroit.

<u>My cousin lives in Detroit.</u>

The man who is standing over there is an Olympic champion.

<u>The man standing over there is an Olympic champion.</u>

1 That's the girl who was beaten in the judo finals last year.

....

2 Did I tell you the joke that Joe told me?

....

3 The story she told us, which was very scary, was about ghosts.

....

4 Did you see that girl who was wearing jeans?

....

5 Those people who are sitting over there are famous athletes.

....

6 I really enjoyed the book that I borrowed from the library.

....

Unit 8 The image industry

1 Making faces

1 Word work: expressions with parts of the face

a Complete the expressions with a part of the face from the box.

| ~~eye~~ eyes (x2) ear ears chin lips |

Could you keep an _eye_ on the baby for five minutes?

1 My .... are sealed. I won't tell a soul.

2 I can't wait to hear your exciting news. I'm all ....

3 Don't worry about your test results. Try to keep your .... up.

4 He was so gorgeous that I couldn't take my .... off him.

5 You never remember what I say. It just goes in one .... and out the other.

6 I'm sure he was making .... at me.

b Match an adjective on the left with a suitable noun on the right to make phrases that describe parts of the face.

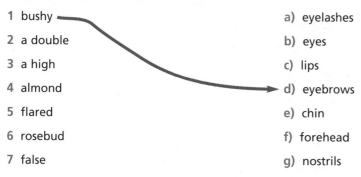

1 bushy a) eyelashes

2 a double b) eyes

3 a high c) lips

4 almond d) eyebrows

5 flared e) chin

6 rosebud f) forehead

7 false g) nostrils

c Use a dictionary to check the meanings of any phrases from exercises 1a and b that you don't know.

2 Skills: reading and writing

a **Read this letter to an advice columnist and make notes about the following.**

the daughter's problems: <u>eats too many snacks</u>

....

possible causes: ....

....

the son's problem: ....

....

the suggested solution: ....

....

> My daughter eats too many snacks between meals but my wife doesn't see it. Teenage angst, studying for her SAT and peer pressure might all be factors but the eating pattern has been consistent. Her grades have been disappointing and she spends a lot of time using the Internet. Her mother refuses to acknowledge this as a problem. Also, my son is anemic. He has a poor diet, is out of school a lot and is unhappy. My wife insists this is psychological and wants us to separate (me to get out) so that the kids see us argue less often. If I thought this would work I would do it, but I feel it would have an irreversible effect. Is there a better solution?

b **Find phrases in the article that mean the same or nearly the same as the following.**

anxiety   <u>angst</u>

1 influence of friends   ....

2 lacking in red blood cells   ....

3 fight   ....

4 cannot be changed   ....

Glossary
SAT: Scholastic Aptitude Test – a test that high school students in the U.S. must take before they can go to college.

c **Write a reply to the letter, suggesting three different courses of action, in three short paragraphs.**

Paragraph 1
suggest making light of the problem – sounds like a normal family situation / will pass as children get older

Paragraph 2
suggest seeking professional help – therapy for daughter / doctor for son
possible benefits and risks involved in this

Paragraph 3
look at the possibility of separation and possible effects, especially on the children

You can begin your letter like this one.

> Dear Mr. X,
> Your situation is probably more common than you realize. As I see it, there are basically three alternative courses of action that you can take. The first is to do ...

2 Cosmetic surgery

1 Skills work: reading

a Read this article and answer the questions.

1 Name three examples of cosmetic surgery mentioned in the article that are inspired by Hollywood stars.

   a) lip enhancing ....

   b) ....

   c) ....

2 What kind of bodies are fashionable in Hollywood?

   ....

3 What is meant by addition and subtraction in this context?

   ....

4 What is a Near Facelift?

   ....

5 What is Tissue Glue used for?

   ....

b Underline all the parts of the body mentioned in the text. Use a dictionary to check the meaning and pronunciation of any words you don't know.

Learning tip

Remember that your own language can help you with your English – many words may be the same or similar. Some, however, may look very similar but may have different meanings.

COSMETIC SURGERY
Los Angeles

THE LATEST LOOK INVOLVES ADDITION AND SUBTRACTION

It's easy to track the next big beauty obsession among the Hollywood elite. Just keep an eye on the movie trailers and award shows. When Angelina Jolie stars in a film, LA types rush to have their lips enhanced. Jennifer Lopez appears in skintight hotpants and buttock liftings soar. Jude Law glistens bare-chested on a beach and hair-removal lasers go into overdrive. Here, the beauty obsession is for a bronzed body without a hair, vein or dimple in sight, and big chests for men and women alike. The look of the moment involves addition and subtraction: fat is taken away from where it doesn't belong and added to where you need it, such as in cheeks, jaws, chins, lips and creases. Dr Peter Bela Fodor in Century City does what he calls a "Near Facelift", utilizing cheek implants and lipocontouring to make you look younger without scarring, and many such operations are being performed every day. In LA, most things are done as a day case and you can be driven home in your convertible a few hours after you arrive. A key innovation is the use of "Tissue Glue", a sticky substance fashioned from your own blood, which speeds up the healing in time for your Oscar to be collected.

c Look at these words from the article. Try to guess what they mean from the context and write a short definition.

obsession   *having something in your mind all the time*

1 elite	.... ○	6 utilizing	.... ○
2 types	.... ○	7 implants	.... ○
3 bronzed	.... ○	8 convertible	.... ○
4 addition	.... ○	9 innovation	.... ○
5 subtraction	.... ○	10 substance	.... ○

d If there is a similar word in your language, try to decide whether the meaning is basically the same or basically different. Write S or D in the appropriate circles, then check in a dictionary.

Language summary: review and extension of passives

Use:	Form:
Use the passive to shift attention from the doer of the action to the receiver. The passive is also used in more formal or more impersonal language. *Patients **are kindly requested** to settle their bill in full after each consultation.*	Simple tenses: receiver + form of *to be* + past participle Cosmetic operations | **are** / **were** | performed | every day. / at that clinic. Progressive tenses: receiver + form of *to be* + *-ing* form + past participle The operation | **is** / **was** | being carried out | at the moment. / when the fire alarm went off. Perfect tenses: receiver + *have / has / had* + form of *to be* + past participle The project | **has** / **had** | been completed | at last. / before we knew about it.

---

2 Language work

a Underline all the examples of the passive used in the text opposite.

b Rewrite these sentences in the passive, using *by* + subject if necessary.

Surgeons at the MacDonald Clinic perform over 20 cosmetic procedures a day.

Over 20 cosmetic procedures a day are performed at the MacDonald Clinic.

1 They have rearranged the facial features of some very famous clients.

....

2 Everyone knows the clinic's reputation for discretion.

....

3 Builders are currently extending the clinic with a new annex.

....

4 The president will open the new annex later this month.

....

3 Selling beauty

1 Word work: words and phrases about advertising

Add one or two words and phrases about advertising to this spidergram, using your own knowledge.

types of product	where seen
clothing	billboard

ADVERTISING

adjectives often used	strategies
wonderful	jingles

2 Skills work: reading

a Read this article quickly and put some more words in the spidergram above.

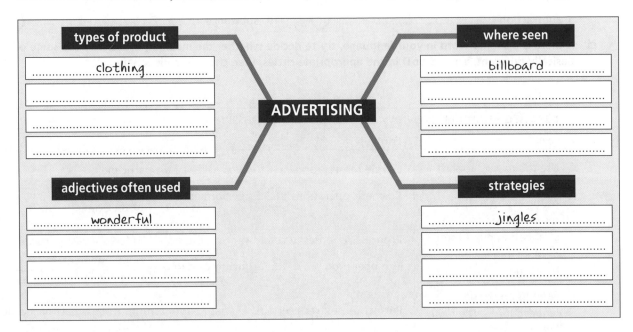

BECAUSE I'M WORTH IT

Women's magazines are crammed with advertisements for cosmetics: makeup, shampoos, conditioners, creams and lotions, all designed to make us look more beautiful, sexier, thinner, younger. If you watch the commercials on TV, rather than using them as an opportunity to get up and replenish your drink, you will notice that again a large proportion of advertising time is taken up by attempts to sell this kind of product.

A number of different strategies or themes are often seen in this kind of advertising.

One is the "before and after" routine, in which two pictures of supposedly the same person are shown, one before and one

after using the product, the contrast providing ample evidence of the miraculous improvement in looks. Then there is the scientific approach, which attempts to convince by using percentages and statistics and words like *tested* and *proven*. Many of these advertisements include or end with a catch phrase that is hard to get out of your mind and that you always associate with the product – at least, that's the theory. One of the best known of these, intended to appeal to the modern woman's sense of pride in herself, is L'Oréal's oft-repeated "because I'm worth it." But what does it mean, I wonder, to be worth the price of a bottle of conditioner?

b **Answer the questions, using a few words only.**

Where can you see a lot of advertisements for cosmetics? ...women's magazines, TV...................................

1 Which strategy uses two pictures? ....

2 Which strategy uses percentages and statistics? ....

3 What should a catch phrase be associated with? ....

4 What does the L'Oréal catch phrase appeal to? ....

5 Does it make sense? Why? / Why not? ....

c **Find words or phrases in the article that mean the same as or something similar to the following.**

packed   ...crammed..........

1 refill   ....

2 efforts   ....

3 apparently ....

4 enough   ....

5 amazing   ....

6 heard frequently ....

Language summary: active and passive

Use:

The passive is often used when we do not know who the subject is, or when the subject is less important than the verb or the object of the active sentence.

*They **are designed** for maximum effect.*

*It **has been said** that time is a great healer.*

---

3 Language work

Look at these examples of the passive from the article. Is it possible to put them in the active? If you think it is possible, rewrite the sentence in the active. You may need to supply a subject for the verb yourself. If you think it is not possible, leave the sentence in the passive.

Women's magazines are crammed with advertisements for cosmetics.

Advertisers cram advertisements for cosmetics into women's magazines...........................

1 The products are all designed to make us look more beautiful.

....

2 A large proportion of advertising time is taken up by attempts to sell this kind of product.

....

3 A number of different strategies are often seen in this kind of advertising.

....

4 Two pictures of the same person are shown.

....

5 The catch phrase is intended to appeal to the modern woman's sense of pride in herself.

....

Unit 9 A question of luck

1 Good and bad luck

1 Skills work: reading

a Look at the headline of this article. Do you think it is about good or bad luck? Write a short prediction about the article.

....

....

b Read the article quickly to check your prediction.

Glossary

nazareno: a member of the religious order of Jesus el Rico

pardon: release from jail or similar removal of punishment, granted officially, e.g. by the president

bubonic plague: a terrible disease, common in the Middle Ages

EASTER TRADITION SETS BANK ROBBER FREE

1 A bank robber walked free from jail last week in Malaga, Spain. Wearing a long black tunic and with a black cloth over his head, he was camouflaged by the hooded nazarenos in the midst of their Holy Week processions.

2 Clemente Perez was the lucky beneficiary of the annual Easter pardon, which is the high point in the week. During this time Seville, Cordoba and Granada are brought almost to a standstill as the various religious groups parade their statues of Jesus and the Virgin Mary through the streets.

3 Clemente Perez was a fisherman who claims to have turned to robbing banks to feed his wife and family. The pardon, which dates back to the time of King Carlos III, will save him five years of a 12-year sentence – provided he does not reoffend.

4 Legend has it that one night prisoners escaped from Malaga prison disguised as nazarenos and paraded a statue of Jesus around the streets. They then performed the miracle of ending an outbreak of the bubonic plague before returning to prison voluntarily.

c Match one of these summaries with each paragraph of the article.

1 description of Holy Week   paragraph ....

2 the origins of the pardon   paragraph ....

3 the prisoner's walk to freedom   paragraph ....

4 the prisoner's background   paragraph ....

d Look at these words and phrases from the article. Try to guess what they mean from the context or from similar words and phrases in your language. Write a short definition.

camouflaged   _hidden by_................................

1 in the midst of ....   4 brought to a standstill ....

2 beneficiary   ....   5 reoffend   ....

3 high point   ....   6 disguised   ....

2 Word work: affixes

a *Reoffend* is an example of adding *re-* before a verb to mean *to do (something) again.*
Write a short sentence to illustrate the meaning of each of these verbs. Use a dictionary to help you.

rebuild   _After the earthquake had destroyed the village, we all rebuilt it._ ....

1 reunite   ....

2 rehouse   ....

3 refill   ....

4 refund   ....

5 reproduce   ....

b Complete these mind maps with appropriate verbs formed with the prefixes and suffixes shown.
Use a dictionary to help you and to check meanings and pronunciation.

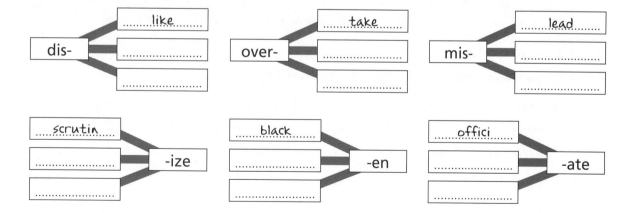

2 Optimism versus pessimism

Language summary: real and unreal conditionals

Use:	Form:

Use:

Use the zero conditional to talk about something that is always or usually true (in a particular set of circumstances).

If people get more exercise, they generally feel healthier.

Use the first conditional to talk about a situation that is possible or likely to happen.
If you go to the gym once a week, you'll probably lose weight.

Use the second conditional to:

- talk about an improbable or unlikely situation in the present or future.
  If I won the lottery, I'd quit my job.

- talk about an impossible or imaginary situation in the present.
  If I were a woman, I'd choose not to have children.

- give advice.
  If I were you, I wouldn't tell him.

Form:

Zero conditional: *if* + subject + present simple, subject + present simple

If	you	**leave** meat out,	it	**turns** rotten.
	we	**go out** to eat,	we	usually **go** to Dino's.

First conditional: *if* + subject + present simple, subject + *will / won't* + verb

If	they	**decide** to visit us,	they	**will call** us first.
	she	**doesn't study** harder,	she	**won't pass** the exam.

Second conditional: *if* + subject + past simple, subject + *would / wouldn't* + verb

If	my dad	**got** that job,	we	**would have to** move.
	you	**weren't** so angry,	you	**would understand**.
	I	**were** you,	I	**wouldn't buy** that car.

Language note

The order of the clauses in conditionals can normally be reversed, and the comma omitted

You'll probably lose weight if you go to the gym once a week.

---

1 Language work

a Match the sentence beginnings on the left with the endings on the right.

1 If you take my advice,	a) he'd probably accept it. ○
2 I wouldn't worry about it	b) we would travel more. ○
3 If we didn't have children,	c) if I were you. ○
4 If she won the lottery,	d) you'll forget what he said. Ⓡ
5 If you don't study,	e) I'd leave him very soon. ○
6 If he were offered the job,	f) she'd give all the money away. ○
7 If I were you,	g) if you heat it. ○
8 Water boils	h) you won't pass the exam. ○

b Decide whether each sentence contains a real condition or an unreal one. Write R or U in the circles.

C **Answer the questions about yourself.**

1 How do you feel during the day if you wake up late?

....

2 What do you do if your boy / girlfriend always arrives late for an evening out?

....

3 If you have some spare time on Saturday, what will you do?

....

4 If you had more time, what new sport would you take up? Why?

....

5 How would you feel if you were offered a job in the United States? Would you take it?

....

2 **Word work:** words and phrases about complaining

Look again at the articles on pages 80 and 81 of your Student's Book.
Find these phrases and then write a short definition or another way of saying each one.

to look on the bright side   <u>to be positive / optimistic</u>

1 to assert your (inalienable) right   ....

2 relentless optimism   ....

3 self-help gurus   ....

4 a good moan   ....

5 to set (absurdly) low expectations   ....

6 to master difficult situations   ....

7 to fear the worst   ....

3 **Skills work:** writing

Correct the mistakes in this text. They may be spelling, punctuation or grammar mistakes.

> Some people says it is a good idea to look in the bright side. Because then you always feel more cheerfull and probably find it easyer to made friends, however there are also people which believes that if you generaly expect the worse you will be more happy. If you think that everything will turns out badly, then the realty should come as a nice sorprise. Things will never be as bad that they are in your imagination.

3 What if …?

1 Skills work: reading

a Look at the headline and subtitle of the article below. What do you think it is about? Write a short prediction about what you will read in the article.

....

b Read the article quickly to check your prediction.

"AIR-RAGE" CASE: NOT GUILTY!

Jury says passenger was defending self during flight

A man was acquitted Tuesday of breaking an airline ticket agent's neck during a scuffle in Newark, NJ, which has come to symbolize "air rage".

Jurors deliberated three and a half hours before clearing John C. Davis Jr. of aggravated assault. The verdict in Essex County Superior Court showed jurors believed that Davis, a steel plant worker from Fredericksburg, Va., acted in self-defense in the incident in July 1999. Davis, 31, sobbed when the verdict was read. If convicted, he could have faced ten years in prison.

The dispute began when Davis and ten other family members began boarding a flight from Newark to Orlando on July 22, 1999, after a two-hour delay. They were on their way to Walt Disney World. Davis' wife, Victoria, testified that Continental Airlines ticket agent Angelo Sottile stopped her from retrieving their 18-month-old daughter, Kayla, who had wandered up a jetway.

Prosecution witnesses said an enraged Davis confronted Sottile for allegedly pushing Victoria, then picked the agent up and slammed him to the ground. Defense witnesses, including Davis and his relatives, insisted that Sottile attacked first by grabbing Davis' neck, and they both fell to the floor after Davis put Sottile in a bear hug.

Sottile was in a coma for five days and has no memory of what happened. He has lost 80% of his neck mobility and now works part-time as a postal worker.

Copyright 2001, USA TODAY. Reprinted with permission.

c Mark these sentences T (true) or F (false).

Davis was found guilty.   T ◯   F ✔

1 The jury thought Davis was provoked.   T ◯   F ◯

2 The plane was late taking off.   T ◯   F ◯

3 Kayla had disappeared.   T ◯   F ◯

4 Davis accused Sottile of pushing Victoria.   T ◯   F ◯

5 Sottile does not remember what happened.   T ◯   F ◯

d In the article there is a useful lexical set about the legal process in court. Underline all the words connected with this in the article, then record them below according to the parts of speech.

Words connected with the legal process

Nouns: ..... case, ...

.....

Verbs: ..... to acquit, ...

Adjectives and adverbs: guilty, ...

> ### Learning tip
> It is always a good idea to record together groups of words and phrases that are related in meaning (lexical sets). In this way, you can always find the words and phrases later on, by looking at topic groups. There are several methods of doing this, e.g. mind maps, word plus definition. You can also record these sets according to parts of speech.

Language summary: unreal conditionals

Use:

Use the third conditional to speculate about how things might have been different.

If we had gotten a taxi, we would have caught the plane.
(= We didn't get a taxi or catch the plane.)

Use a third conditional to speculate how things might be different now.

If we hadn't met, I wouldn't be so happy now. (= We did meet and I am happy now.)

Form:

Third conditional: *if* + past perfect, *would /wouldn't* + present perfect

If	we	**had stayed** in that hotel,	we	**would**	**have died.**
	you	**hadn't taken** the new job,	you	**would**	**have gotten** a raise.

Mixed conditional: *if* + past perfect, *would /wouldn't* + verb

If	we	**had stayed** in that hotel,	we	**would be** dead now.
	you	**hadn't taken** the new job,	you	**would be** a manager now.

2 Language work

Make sentences speculating about the article, using the unreal conditionals.

jury / not believe Davis, be / jail now

If the jury hadn't believed Davis, he would be in jail now.

1 jury / convict him, go / jail for ten years

.....

2 Kayla / not wander / jetway, Victoria / not try to retrieve her

.....

3 Sottile / not push Victoria, fight / not happen

.....

4 Davis and Sottile / be sensible, Sottile / not lose his memory

.....

5 Sottile / not lose his memory, not be / postal worker now

.....

Unit 10 Free time

1 Blood sports

1 Skills work: reading

Camel wrestling

One of the most popular spectator sports in south-western Turkey is camel wrestling. Although it is not strictly a blood sport since the animals are rarely seriously hurt, camel wrestling can involve bruising and bloody noses, and is clearly an example of animals being exploited by humans for their own pleasure and entertainment.

Camels used to be the main means of transportation in the Middle East and in some regions they are still used in this way.

Camel wrestling is said to date back to a time when herdsmen noticed that male camels would fight over female camels during the mating season. The herdsmen spotted an opportunity to turn this into a sport.

Nowadays, the sport centers on the town of Selcuk, where tournaments are held every weekend from January to March in a carnival atmosphere. For many, this represents big business, as members of the public bet on their favorite camel and set up stalls selling carpets and handicrafts.

During the fight itself two male camels, each weighing over a ton and standing over two meters at its hump, wrestle over a female camel who is brought in to arouse their excitement and jealousy. They charge at one another and one tries to crush the other with its weight before they are pulled apart with rope, tug-of-war style. To win, one camel has to knock the other down on his side, chase him out of the stadium or make him squeal. Otherwise, the match is a draw.

a Read the article and answer the questions.

Why isn't camel wrestling strictly a blood sport?

<u>Because the camels are not usually seriously hurt.</u>

1 What were camels originally used for?

....

2 How did camel wrestling begin?

....

3 How is money made on camel wrestling?

....

4 What role does the female play in the fight?

....

5 How is the match won?

....

b Find words or phrases in the article that match these definitions.

a sport that people watch   a̲ ̲s̲p̲e̲c̲t̲a̲t̲o̲r̲ ̲s̲p̲o̲r̲t̲   **3** the period of sexual activity in animals   ....

1 used (usually for profit)   ....   **4** a mood of celebration and enjoyment   ....

2 a method of getting around   ....   **5** to provoke a feeling in someone   ....

2 Word work: expressions of agreement and disagreement

Look at these ways of agreeing and disagreeing. Write them in the correct column in order of strength: the strongest at the top and the weakest at the bottom.

> I'm not sure I agree with you.   ~~Absolutely~~!   I disagree.   You can't be serious!   Nonsense!
>
> I see what you mean.   You're right.   I do agree with you.   I'm not sure about that but …
>
> I don't think that's true at all.

Agreeing	Disagreeing
Absolutely!	

3 Pronunciation work: homophones

a These words each have a homophone: a word that sounds the same but is spelled differently. Write the alternative spelling underneath each word. Use a dictionary to help you if necessary.

weather   D̲o̲ ̲y̲o̲u̲ ̲t̲h̲i̲n̲k̲ ̲t̲h̲e̲ ̲w̲e̲a̲t̲h̲e̲r̲'̲s̲ ̲g̲o̲i̲n̲g̲ ̲t̲o̲ ̲b̲e̲ ̲g̲o̲o̲d̲ ̲t̲h̲i̲s̲ ̲w̲e̲e̲k̲e̲n̲d̲?̲

w̲h̲e̲t̲h̲e̲r̲   I̲ ̲d̲o̲n̲'̲t̲ ̲k̲n̲o̲w̲ ̲w̲h̲e̲t̲h̲e̲r̲ ̲I̲ ̲c̲a̲n̲ ̲c̲o̲m̲e̲ ̲t̲o̲ ̲t̲h̲e̲ ̲m̲o̲v̲i̲e̲ ̲t̲o̲n̲i̲g̲h̲t̲ ̲o̲r̲ ̲n̲o̲t̲.̲

1 fair   ....

....

2 peace   ....

....

3 plane   ....

....

4 which   ....

....

5 cereal   ....

....

6 principle   ....

....

b Write a sentence for each homophone that clearly illustrates its meaning.

Unit 10 Lesson 2

2 A game of skill and luck

1 Word work: words and phrases about games

a Can you name one or more games in which you:

1 use counters? ....

2 have a king? ....

3 buy and sell property? ....

4 roll dice? ....

5 have trumps? ....

6 play with a partner? ....

b The following are all expressions from games that have a metaphorical meaning. Match the expressions with their meanings. Use a dictionary if necessary.

1 to follow suit   a) it's not possible

2 an opening gambit   b) to be likely to happen

3 poker-faced   c) to do the same thing

4 to be in the cards   d) to behave in such a way that you get what you want

5 no dice   e) the thing you do or say first

6 to play your cards right   f) expressionless

Language summary: instructions

Use:	Form:
Instructions commonly use: imperatives (with or without you) **You deal** the cards to all the players. **Don't look** at the cards yet.	Imperative: positive (*you*) + verb negative *don't* + verb (You) **Look** at your cards. / **Miss** a turn. Don't **look** at your cards. / **miss** a turn.
modal verbs (e.g. *must, mustn't, can*) Your partner then **has to** play. You **mustn't** communicate with him or her.	Modal verbs: subject + modal verb + verb We have to / mustn't / should add our points together.
if clauses and *when* clauses **If** you can't go, you miss a turn. **When** all the cards are gone, the game is over.	*If / When* clauses: *if / when* + subject + verb, main clause **If** you have a six, start the game. **When** she has a six, she can start the game.

60

2 Language work

a Write these instructions in the correct column.

~~Take turns to roll the dice.~~   You have to deal the cards.   Don't shuffle between games.

If you want, you can play in pairs.   You must move your counters around the board.

You can move any piece you want.   You can choose to miss a turn.   You have to follow suit.

You mustn't communicate with your partner.   When you finish, you can pick up another card.

Things you must do	Things you can do	Things you mustn't do
Take turns to roll the dice.		

b Here are the instructions for a simple card game. Number them 1–6 in the correct order.

.... Then the dealer deals the cards out – 7 per player and 8 for the dealer.

.... If a player can't go, they pick up a card from the deck.

.... The dealer starts the game by putting any card face up on the table.

.... The first player to use all their cards is the winner.

...1... First, someone shuffles the cards – this person is the dealer.

.... Other players have to follow either with the same suit or the same number.

3 Skills work: writing

a Choose a board game or card game you are familiar with and write information about it.

Name of the game: ....

Aim of the game: ....

Number of players: ....

Equipment needed: ....

How the game starts: ....

What you have to do: ....

What you mustn't do: ....

What you can do if you want to: ....

How the game is won: ....

b Explain the game for someone who has never played before. Write two paragraphs.

Paragraph 1: describe the game – its aims, equipment, etc.

Paragraph 2: describe the rules of the game and how it is won.

3 Let's get together

1 Skills work: reading

a Look at the picture, the title and the subtitle of this article. Try to predict some words that you will read in the article.

....

b Read the article quickly and check your predictions.

COFFEE TO GO – ALL OVER THE GLOBE

Can U.S. gourmet coffee chain Starbucks convert Continental Europe's café society? It's ready to try.

In the U.S., hardly anyone under 25 refers to "one-horse towns" any more. Oh, these small, boring places still exist. But today they're usually called something else: "one-Starbucks towns", in a nod to the gourmet coffee chain that is making its mark worldwide.

Continental Europeans have recently been able to see for themselves what all the fuss is about. Though Starbucks has been in Britain since 1998, it steamed into Zürich last month with the first of 50-plus outlets planned for Switzerland. With its multicultural and multilingual population, the country provides a "tremendous opportunity to learn how to operate elsewhere in Europe," says Mark McKeon, president of Starbucks Europe, Middle East and Africa. By the end of next year, the company intends to have outlets in Germany, France, Spain and – significantly – Italy, where Starbucks' chairman Howard Schultz found the inspiration for a chain of espresso bars. To achieve its stated objective of "establishing Starbucks as the most recognized and respected brand in the world," the company is rapidly opening stores around the globe – at an average of three a day.

Since its start in Seattle three decades ago, Starbucks has become one of the great marketing success stories in recent memory. Positioning itself as the descendant of the 19th century coffeehouse, but with latte, Starbucks is a lifestyle choice for urban sophisticates. Even British Prime Minister Tony Blair was moved to declare after a visit to a central London outlet last year that "the Starbucks experience seems to epitomize all that is modern in a democratic society." In the U.S., as well as in 20 other countries, "Starbucks has revolutionized what was a traditional industry," says Jeffrey Young, managing director of the retail consultancy Allegra Consultants. "It has made coffee drinking fashionable again."

c These are the answers to questions about the article. Read it again and write the questions.

"One-Starbucks towns."

What are small, boring towns in the U.S. usually called now?
....

1 Because the population is multicultural and multilingual.
....

2 In Italy.
....

3 To establish Starbucks as the most recognized and respected brand in the world.
....

4 Nineteenth-century coffeehouses.
....

Language summary: adverbs and adverbials

Use:	Form:
Use adverbs and adverbials to qualify verbs and adjectives and give information about: • how (manner) *She drove **carelessly**.* • how often (frequency) *They **never** go out.* • when (time) *They're getting married **next year**.* • where (place) *The bathroom's **upstairs**.* • how much (degree) *I **hardly** know him.*	Adverbs of manner are single words. They are usually formed by adding -*ly* to an adjective and they usually follow the verb. Adverbs of frequency are single words. They usually precede the verb, except in the case of *to be* and modal verbs, which they follow. Adverbs and adverbials of time and place can be single words or phrases. They usually come either at the beginning or at the end of the sentence. Adverbs of degree are usually single words. They usually precede the verb, except in the case of *to be* and modal verbs, which they follow.

---

2 Language work

These adverbs and adverbials come from the article about Starbucks. Write them in the correct column below.

~~hardly~~ today worldwide recently next year significantly rapidly last year

Manner	Frequency	Time	Place	Degree
				hardly

Unit 11 Furry friends

1 Preservation or extinction?

1 Word work: expressions with animals

snail	horse	hawk	sheep	fish
	monkey	~~dog~~	bull	

a Complete these sentences with the name of an animal from the box.

Don't go an see that terrible movie. It's a real ..dog..!

1 She drinks like a .... – nearly a bottle of wine a day!

2 How can you see that from here? You must have eyes like a ....

3 I'm so hungry I could eat a ....

4 I thought I told you not to .... around with that computer.

5 You just have to be brave and take the .... by the horns.

6 Sorry we're late. The traffic was moving at a .... 's pace.

7 My sister's the black .... of the family. She ran away at 16 to marry an older man.

b Use a dictionary to check the meaning of any expressions you're not sure about.

c In English, there are a lot of expressions with *cat* and *dog*. One of the best known, though rarely used, is *It's raining cats and dogs*. Use a dictionary to look up expressions with *cat* and *dog*. Choose three with each animal that you like and write them in the chart, then write a sentence to show the meaning of each one.

let the cat out of the bag ....

....

....

....

....

....

We wanted to throw Mom a surprise birthday party, but someone let the cat out of the bag.

1 ....

2 ....

3 ....

4 ....

5 ....

2 Skills work: writing – using linking and sequencing devices

a Look at these devices used for linking and sequencing from your Student's Book.

> In our opinion, ...   Above all, ...   First, ...   Therefore, ...   Furthermore, ...   Finally, ...

To present different points in an argument, we can also use:

Firstly, ...   Secondly, ...   Finally, ...

The activities in the chart are often considered to put animals at risk of extinction. Complete the chart with reasons why they put animals at risk.

Activity	Why animals are at risk
overfishing	decreases fish stocks in the ocean
	removes food of bigger fish and mammals, e.g. sharks
hunting	
river and ocean pollution	
destroying rain forests and other habitats	
trading in animal goods, e.g. skins, ivory	

b Now write a paragraph about the dangers of extinction to some animal species. Include:

which activities put animals at risk and why

your feelings about this

what we can do to avoid some animals becoming extinct

Start like the example, and try to use some of the sequencers above in your paragraph.

> The possible extinction of some animal species is a genuine cause for concern nowadays. A number of activities put animals at risk. First, overfishing oceans is a real problem because it decreases fish stocks in the ocean and removes the food of bigger animals, such as sharks. Second, ...

2 Responsible ownership

1 Skills work: reading

a Read this letter to a problem page about pets and answer the questions.

> *Dear Annie,*
>
> *Some friends of mine have a really tricky problem and I thought I'd write and ask your advice. They have two German shepherds. They're big dogs and they're getting on in years, but they're both very active and they need to be walked at least twice a day. The problem is that these friends have recently had a baby, and the other day one of the dogs went for him. Although this wasn't a serious attack, my friends now feel that it is too risky to keep the dogs in the house and they have put them in a kennel. This is distressing my friends, as well as costing them a huge amount of money.*
>
> *What should they do? Should they leave the dogs in the kennel, where no one really loves them and it's costing a lot? My friends really don't want to have the dogs put to sleep because they love them and they still have a lot of life left. However, it will be hard to find a new owner because the dogs are pretty old and they should be kept together. Please can you suggest anything?*
>
> *Yours sincerely,*
>
> *Jake Jones*

What are the dogs like? <u>They're big and they're active but they're getting on in years.</u>

1 Why do the friends need to get rid of the dogs? ....

2 Where are the dogs now? ....

3 Are the owners happy about the situation? ....

4 Why will it be hard to find new owners? ....

b Look at these words and phrases from the article. Try to guess what they mean from the context or from similar words and phrases in your language. Write a synonym or a short definition.

tricky <u>complicated</u> ....

1 getting on in years ....

2 went for ....

3 risky ....

4 kennel ....

5 distressing ....

6 put to sleep ....

2 Skills work: writing

Look at this reply to Jake Jones. The writer has not punctuated it or put it into paragraphs. Rewrite it to include punctuation and paragraphs.

> dear jake thank you for your letter about your friends problem with their dogs it sounds like a very difficult problem and not one i would like to have to deal with myself but ill try to give you some advice first i think you should ask your friends if they have advertised there may be someone who would like these dogs but they need to reach that person through advertising they could try local stores or the internet if that doesnt work they could try advertising in the local newspaper an alternative would be to take the dogs to a dog pound and hope that from there some new owners can be found i hope you find these suggestions useful and wish your friends luck yours sincerely annie

Language summary: *hope* and *wish*

Use:

We use *hope*:

- to talk about a desire in the future, i.e. something that may happen
  I **hope** she arrives soon. We don't want to miss the beginning of the movie.

- to express a desire that a past event has taken place
  I **hope** Jeff remembered to mail my application form.

We use *wish*:

- to express regrets about the present, to talk about things that are unlikely to change
  I **wish** I lived in Santa Barbara.

- to express a desire for a present event or situation to change, to express impatience or annoyance with another person
  I **wish** we could live by the ocean.
  I **wish** he would quit smoking.

- to express regrets about the past, to talk about past events or situations that can't change
  I **wish** you hadn't told me about Mel; I can't look her in the face now.

Form:

Future desire: subject + *hope* + (*that*) + subject + present simple or *will / won't* + verb

| She | **hopes** | (that) | her test results | **arrive** tomorrow. |
| We | **hope** | | you and your friend | **will be able** to join us. |

Desire about the past: subject + *hope* + (*that*) + subject + past simple or present perfect

| I | **hope** | (that) **you** | **haven't forgotten** to make the reservation. |
| We | | | **had** a pleasant flight last week. |

Present regret: subject + *wish* + (*that*) + subject + past simple or *were / weren't*

| He | **wishes** (that) | she | **lived** closer to him. |
| She | | he | **weren't** in love with someone else. |

Desire for something to change: subject + *wish* + (*that*) + subject + *could / couldn't* + verb

OR subject + *wish* + (*that*) + different subject + *would / wouldn't* + verb

| I | **wish** | (that) | I | **could sing** better. |
| They | | | we | **would stop** playing loud music. |

Past regret: subject + *wish* + (*that*) + subject + past perfect

| We | **wish** | (that) | we | **hadn't bought** this house. |
| She | **wishes** | | she | **had gone** to college. |

3 Language work

Rewrite these sentences to correct the mistakes. Do not change either *wish* or *hope*.

I wish I didn't buy the cat but it's too late now. _I wish I hadn't bought the cat._

1 I hope you would find an owner for my dog. ....

2 I wish I can have a dog but I can't because my apartment is too small. ....

3 I wish my apartment is bigger. ....

4 She hopes he had remembered to call the vet. ....

5 I wish he will train the dog to sit. ....

3 Animals as healers and teachers

1 Skills work: reading

a Read the article and answer the questions.

Why do you think Greenwich has a theater cat? *Maybe the cat catches mice in the theater.*

1 What happened to the last one? ....

2 Where was Herbie found? ....

3 Why do you think the theater closed in 1998? ....

4 How will Herbie be paid for? ....

5 Why is this necessary? ....

Welcome back cat

Greenwich Theater (in London) has reinstated the post of "Official Theater Cat" and appointed a two-year-old tomcat called Herbie.

Television and theater star, Prunella Scales, welcomed the new recruit and helped settle him into his new quarters. The Theater Director, Hilary Strong, said: "Greenwich has always had a theater cat. When the theater closed in 1998 the last incumbent was retired to the country, but now we are open again, we are delighted to be able to adopt a cat from Battersea Dogs' Home." She said Herbie had settled in well and enjoyed wandering around the backstage area.

Cash-strapped Greenwich Theater will not have to worry about the cost of caring for Herbie, as a unique sponsorship deal has been struck with the firm Pets at Home, who have agreed to provide food, litter, veterinary treatments and toys. Prunella Scales is a great cat lover and is looking forward to meeting up with Herbie when she returns to Greenwich in April with her new play, *The External*.

Glossary

Battersea Dogs' Home: a center in south London for stray or unwanted dogs and cats

b Find words or phrases in the article that mean the same as or something similar to the following.

put something back in place, e.g. a job *reinstate*

1 job, position ....

2 someone recently joined ....

3 accommodations ....

4 person holding a post ....

5 not having much money ....

6 dry material used in a cat's indoor toilet ....

Language summary: mixed conditionals

Use:	Form:
We use a variety of combinations of tenses to talk about conditions and consequences. Here are some common mixed conditionals.	
• to ask about present willingness *If you'll cook tonight, I'll do the dishes.*	*if + will / won't* + verb, *will / won't* + verb If you **won't go** to bed now, **I won't let** you watch TV tomorrow.
• to express a past consequence of a present condition (real or imaginary) *If that is the case, they have lied.* *If they liked opera, they would have gone yesterday.*	*if + present simple, present perfect* If this task **is** too difficult, then you **haven't trained** him well enough. *if + past simple (or were), would / wouldn't +* present perfect If I **were** you, I **wouldn't have gone** on vacation with her.
• to express a present consequence of a past condition *If he hadn't robbed the bank, he wouldn't be in prison.*	*if + past perfect, would / wouldn't* + verb If my mother **hadn't called** you, you **wouldn't know** about my illness.
• to express a future consequence of a past condition *If you've all finished, I'll clear up the dirty dishes.*	*if + present perfect, will / wouldn't* + verb If you**'ve** all **finished** writing, **I'll collect** the exam papers.
• to deduce a past consequence of a present condition *If she's at home today, then she didn't go / hasn't gone to New York.*	*if + present simple, past simple / present perfect* If you **don't hear** from me, then **I haven't been able** to contact the theater.

2 Language work

Complete this conversation with the appropriate conditionals (mixed and traditional).

A: I'll ..get.. (get) the drinks if you **(1)** .... (find a seat).

B: OK. I'll find somewhere to sit by the window.

A: Did I tell you I'm thinking about getting a pet.

B: Are you. What kind?

A: Well, I can't really decide. If what you said about dogs is true, it **(2)** .... (be) better to get a cat. Dogs need too much care and attention.

B: I'm not sure about that. Cats need care too. Imagine, if you **(3)** .... (have) a cat, you **(4)** .... (not be able) to go away easily.

A: Yeah, I guess, but if I **(5)** .... (ask) my neighbors, I'm sure they **(6)** .... (take care of) it.

B: I wouldn't be so sure. You know what happened to my cat once? It was a nightmare.

A: What?

B: Well, I went away for a week once and asked a friend to feed it and she completely forgot to! If she **(7)** .... (not be) normally such a reliable person, I **(8)** .... (not ask) her. But this time she really let me down.

A: What happened?

B: Luckily the neighbors heard this awful meowing and called my hotel. I had to cut my trip short. If I **(9)** .... (not go) home immediately, I don't think the cat **(10)** .... (be) alive today.

A: Wow! Well, that's put me off the idea of a pet.

B: Good. If I **(11)** .... (put you off), you **(12)** .... (thank) me in the end.

Unit 12 Using language skills

1 Read to learn

1 Skills work: reading

a Think about all the things you read yesterday, including things like advertisements and labels, both in English and in your own language. Make a list.

....

Did you notice any differences in the ways you read these things? What?

....

b Look at the title of this text. Make a prediction of what might be mentioned in it.

....

c Read through the text quickly and check your prediction.

Reasons to read, strategies for reading

There are many different reasons for reading and many different ways of actually approaching a text. Probably the most common reason for reading is to acquire information or knowledge – think of the number of hours people spend on the Internet browsing for interesting tidbits or investigating a specific topic in depth. A great deal of reading is also done for pleasure, and these two reasons – acquiring knowledge and pleasure – are of course not mutually exclusive. In other words, you can read a novel for entertainment and pick up some useful knowledge about, say, a particular period of history on the way.

The way you approach a text will vary according to your main reason for reading it. If you want to find out what a text is about, you'll skim it quickly. Most people reading for pleasure also read fairly quickly, perhaps skipping parts that seem less appealing or because they just can't wait to see what befalls their favorite character. Some people even read the end of a novel before they are halfway through, and then somehow push their stolen knowledge to the back of their minds. If the text is more challenging, perhaps because it is literary, or an older text somewhat archaic in style or in a foreign language, people tend to read more slowly and spend time thinking about and savoring the words and expressions.

One kind of text that many people still read on a daily basis is a newspaper. A common approach to this is to skim through quickly to find out about the main items of news, then perhaps scan a few articles to extract the most important points. After that – maybe even later on in the day – you might settle down to some more in-depth reading of a number of articles, probably selected with the help of headlines and pictures to guide you toward topics that interest you or arouse your curiosity.

d Mark the sentences T (true) or F (false).

The most common reason for reading is entertainment. T ◯ F ☑

1 Reading for knowledge and reading for pleasure always overlap. T ◯ F ◯

2 Many people leave out parts of novels. T ◯ F ◯

3 It takes more time to read literature than lighter books. T ◯ F ◯

4 Headlines can help you decide whether to read an article or not. T ◯ F ◯

e Look at these words and phrases from the article. Try to guess what they mean from the context or from similar words or phrases in your language. Write a short definition.

acquire ......get......

1 browsing .... 2 tidbits .... 3 in-depth .... 4 mutually exclusive ....

5 skip .... 6 befalls .... 7 archaic .... 8 savoring ....

f Check your definitions in a dictionary. Then check the meaning and pronunciation of any other words and phrases you are not sure about and record any that you want to remember.

2 Learner training: strategies for reading in the future

a The following are stages that you might go through when reading any short text. You have just gone through these stages with the above text – but not in this order. Look at the stages and number them in the correct order, according to what you have just done with the text above.

.... Look at unknown words in the text and try to work out their meaning from the context.

.... Skim through the text to get a general idea of what it is about.

.... Check the meanings of unknown words in a dictionary.

...1... Think about what you know about the topic and try to predict some of the content of the text.

.... Record any words and phrases that are of interest to you.

.... Read the text for more specific information / detail.

This order is not rigid of course, but if you follow these stages sometimes, it will help you get the most out of your reading in the future. You can even set yourself some questions that you would like to find answered by the text and use these when reading for more specific information / detail – although you will not necessarily find the answers, of course.

b Find a text in English that interests you and that you have not read before. Try out the above procedure with your chosen text.

2 Writing in the right tone

1 Skills work: reading

a Below are the parts of a formal letter and an e-mail, but they are mixed up and in the wrong order. Separate the letter and the e-mail and put them in the right order. Mark the letter with the numbers 1–8 and the e-mail with the letters A–G.

.... I therefore feel I have no alternative but to resign.

.... I do hope you will understand the reasons I have given and release me as soon as possible.

.... I look forward to hearing from you.

.... Best wishes, Roger.

.... I am writing to inform you that I wish to tender my resignation.

.... Hope all's well. Hear from you soon.

.... I've just finished the report, thank heaven, and I'll be sending it soon.

.... Thought I'd just send a quick message to update you.

..A.. Hi, Sam, how's it going?

.... Yours sincerely, John Brunswick

.... Hope yours is going OK – send it ASAP so I can have a quick look.

.... Unfortunately, recent events at the office have caused me a great deal of stress,

..!.. Dear Ms. Kramer,

.... Before I go – just had an e-mail from Jo. She's fine and sends love.

.... and I feel I have not been sufficiently supported by my supervisor.

b Answer these questions about the completed letter and e-mail.

Who is the letter to? <u>Ms. Kramer (possibly a personnel manager)</u>

1 What is the relationship between Sam and Roger? ....

2 What is the main purpose of the letter? ....

3 What is the main purpose of the e-mail? ....

4 Why is John Brunswick resigning? ....

5 Who do you think Jo is? ....

2 **Skills:** writing

a Look back at the letter and the e-mail. Underline any words or expressions that show the level of formality in each case.

b Write a summary of the features of formal writing and the features of informal writing by completing the outline.

In formal writing <u>we do not use contractions</u> ....

....

In informal writing ....

....

c Here is an e-mail sent from someone in an office to a colleague. Convert the e-mail into a formal letter from the conference organizer.

> ▷ Attachments: *none*
> 🔳 | Verdana ▾ | Medium ▾ | **B** *I* <u>U</u> T | ≣ ≣ ≣ | ⌸ ⌸ ⌸ ⌸ | **A** ▾ 🖎 ▾ | ▬
>
> Hello, Carol, thought I'd send you some info about the conference. It's from April 12-15,
>
> starts at 9:00 every day and should finish around 6:00.
>
> Looks pretty interesting – lots of good talks on – program attached.
>
> Let me know ASAP if you want to go. Ciao, Frank

3 **Learner training:** strategies for writing in the future

Remember that when you write, you do not normally put pen to paper immediately, but you prepare before you start writing. Here are some steps you can follow when you are writing a piece in English (or in your own language), especially if it is a creative or imaginative piece. Number the steps in a logical order.

.... Put your notes in some kind of order; think about what will go in each paragraph.

.... Write a first draft, thinking about your audience. Who are you writing to or for?

.... Make some notes on anything you might include.

..1... Think about what you know about the subject and what you want to say.

.... Write your final draft.

.... Proofread your work very carefully: use a dictionary / grammar book to check anything you're not sure about.

3 The art of listening

1 Skills work: thinking about listening

Answer the questions about yourself.

1 What kind of things do you listen to on a
   regular basis in your own language? In English?

   ....

   ....

   ....

2 How is listening in your own language different from listening in English?

   ....

   ....

3 What kind of things do you find difficult about listening in English?

   ....

   ....

4 What strategies can you use to help yourself?

   ....

   ....

5 What can you do when you don't understand something you have heard?

   ....

   ....

2 Word work: expressions for asking for clarification

a **When you are listening to a person talking, you can stop them and ask for repetition or clarification. You
can also check that you've understood details and summarize the main points to check your understanding.
These are all phrases you can use to do these things. Put them in the correct column of the table opposite.**

   I'm sorry. Could you say that again, please?

   I'd like to be sure that I have the details right. Did you say ...?

   I'm afraid I don't know what X means? Could you explain?

   Excuse me. I didn't quite catch that. What was it again?

   So, if I understood correctly, we begin at ...

   Could you run through the dates and times again, please?

   Sorry, I'm not sure what you mean.

   As I understand it, you're going to ...

   I'm afraid I don't quite understand. Could you repeat that, please?

Repetition	Clarification
I'm sorry, could you say that again, please?	

Checking details	Summarizing

b Think about the stress and intonation of these expressions – you want to sound as polite as possible. Practice saying them to yourself.

3 Learner training: strategies for listening in the future

a What could you listen to in English? What is available in your home? In your hometown? Write a list of all the available things you can listen to in English.

....

....

b Think about strategies you can use to help you develop your listening skills in the future. Here are some suggestions to help you. Check (✔) the strategies you already use.

Use visual clues as much as possible. ◯

Try not to get stuck on unknown words. Move on and try to follow what is being said. ◯

If you can, record things so that you can listen to them several times. ◯

Set yourself some tasks / questions before you listen to help you focus. If you can't think of

anything, take notes while you listen. ◯

If you are watching a movie with subtitles, try only to read them when you need to check something. ◯

Practice using the phrases in exercise 2 when you are having a conversation. ◯

If you like songs, use them to help you with your listening. Each time you listen, try to understand

more of the words. If you have a copy of the lyrics, you can read this while you listen. ◯

Now try to use some of the strategies that you haven't checked.

A Learner training

1 Using a dictionary

One of the most useful sources of information about the English language is a monolingual (English / English) dictionary. You can greatly improve your reading skills and increase your vocabulary if you learn to use such a dictionary efficiently. Below is a typical dictionary entry. To get the most out of your dictionary, you need to know what is included and what each part means.

| 1 the definition | 2 the phonetic transcription | 3 related expressions using the word |

language / ˈlæŋgwɪdʒ / *n* **1** [U] the system of communication used by people to express ideas, thoughts and feelings, consisting of sounds and words: *It is fascinating to watch the development of language in young children.* **2** [C] the language system used by the people of a country: *He speaks four foreign languages as well as his own language.*

bad language offensive language, swearing: *Don't use such bad language to your mother.*

speak the same language to have similar opinions and / or attitudes: *I think we can do business; we speak the same language.*

4 the stress mark

8 the head word

7 the part of speech

5 the example

6 information about whether the word is countable or uncountable

Task 1
Label the parts of the dictionary entry by drawing lines from the labels above to the correct part.
Try to get into the habit of using this information when you look up a word or phrase.

Task 2
Get to know your dictionary! We all know what a dictionary is, but do we know exactly what it contains? Depending on which dictionary you have, you may be able to find any or all of the following:

a phonemic alphabet .... an irregular verb table .... information about grammar ....

information about affixation (word-building) .... information about punctuation ....

information about spelling rules .... information about parts of speech ....

differences between British and American English ....

false friends (words/phrases which appear very similar in your language and English but in fact have a

different meaning) ....

Look at your dictionary and try to find each of the above. Write the page number(s) next to the item.
Add any other items that you find, with the page number(s). If you can't find many of these items in your dictionary, it may be time to buy a new one!

Suggested answers	8 language	4 ˈ
	7 *n*	3 bad language / speak the same language
	6 [U]	2 / ˈlæŋgwɪdʒ/
	5 It is fascinating ...	1 the system of ...
		Task 1

2 More ways of recording new vocabulary

Throughout *Skyline* you have been shown ways of recording vocabulary. You should continue to record vocabulary systematically through your English learning and review what you have recorded every so often, for example, once a week.

It is important to record as much information as you can about each new word or phrase, rather like the dictionary definition opposite, but perhaps not in quite so much detail! This will help you to use the word or phrase accurately later. Aspects of the word or phrase you can include in your recording are:

• a definition, translation or example to illustrate the meaning (or a combination of these)

• the part of speech

• phrases to show what words / type of word it regularly collocates (combines) with

• something about the pronunciation, especially word stress

This may all seem rather laborious, but the more work you do with a new word or phrase, the more likely you are to remember it.

Task 1
Record these words and phrases, including some of the features mentioned above.
astronomical prices   disapprove   commiserate   hideous   overview

You can record a lot of new vocabulary with a spidergram. This works particularly well with lexical sets: words or phrases about a topic, which are related in meaning. We are more likely to remember things in associated groups than in isolation. Here is an example:

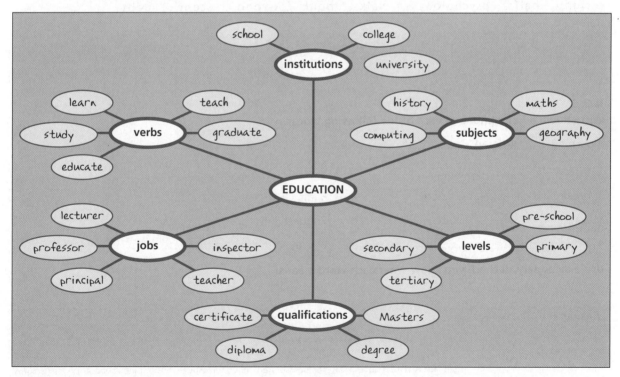

Task 2
Make a spidergram of your own about the topic of housing.

B Spelling rules / word order

1 Sound and spelling relationships

Task 1

Write down some words which illustrate some of the different ways *-ough* can be pronounced. Use a dictionary to help you.

through /θru:/

....

Task 2

Circle the silent letter(s) in each of these words.

thum(b)   knife   scissors   whisper   should   castle   handsome

resign   half   psychology   walk   hour   wrong   scene   debt

Task 3

Write down a homophone of each of the following words.

mourning   morning

1 threw   ....

2 break   ....

3 way   ....

4 aloud   ....

5 road   ....

6 air   ....

7 guest   ....

8 pray   ....

Use a dictionary to check you know what each word means.

2 Multi-word verbs

> There are a lot of examples of multi-word verbs in English and they can be quite difficult to understand and even more difficult to use yourself. A multi-word verb is a phrase which consists of a verb + an adverb / preposition or a combination of these. There are several different types.
>
> | Type 1 | Intransitive verbs + adverb: *She saw the blood and **passed out**.* This type has no object. |
> | --- | --- |
> | Type 2 | Transitive verbs + adverb: *He **put** the dinner things / them **away**.* *He **put away** the dinner things.* This type can be separated by the object. |
> | Type 3 | Transitive verb + preposition: *They **looked after** the children / them.* The two parts cannot be separated by an object. |
> | Type 4 | Transitive verb + adverb + preposition: *She **gets along** well **with** her sister.* The three parts cannot be separated by an object. |

Task 1
Rewrite these sentences, using a suitable multi-word verb.

I really can't tolerate this loud music any longer.

I really can't put up with this loud music any longer.   type 4

1 I tried to find it in the dictionary.

....

2 The fire alarm rang at 8:30.

....

3 He robbed a bank and escaped without punishment.

....

4 I just can't seem to recover from this terrible flu.

....

5 That dress really matches your jacket.

....

Task 2
Which type in the chart does each verb belong to? Write type 1, 2 3, or 4 next to your answers.

Answers

Task 1 and 2

1 I tried to look it up in the dictionary. (type 2)
2 The fire alarm went off at 8.30. (type 1)
3 He robbed a bank and got away with it. (type 4)
4 I just can't seem to get over this terrible flu. (type 4)
5 That dress really goes with your jacket. (type 3)

Macmillan Education
Between Towns Road, Oxford OX4 3PP
A division of Macmillan Publishers Limited
Companies and representatives throughout the world

ISBN 978 0 333 92761 8

Text © Macmillan Publishers Limited 2002
Design and illustration © Macmillan Publishers Limited 2002

First published 2002

Designed by Oliver Hickey
Illustrated by Martin Aston, Maureen Gray, Andy Warrington and
Geoff Waterhouse.
Cover photograph by Stone

The authors and publishers would like to thank the following for
permission to reproduce their material: *Astérix sure has Gaul* by
Bruce Crumley in *Time International* 9th April 2001 © 2001 Time
Inc. Reprinted by permission; Adapted text from *See yourself in
cyberspace* in *Time International* 18th December 2000 © 2000
Time Inc. Reprinted by permission; Illustration from *See yourself in
cyberspace* © Jay Coneyl. Reprinted by permission; Extracts from *Let
them eat fries* by Erika Buck in *Time International* 18th December
2000 © 2000 Time Inc. Reprinted by permission; Film review from
Girl About Town 2nd April 2001. Reprinted by permission of Dee
Pilgrim the compiler; Extracts from *He's beyond music, beyond
lyrics* from Features in *The Guardian* 25th March 2001 © The
Guardian 2001. Reprinted by permission of Guardian Newspapers
Limited; Extracts from *Cincinnati mayor declares curfew after
second night of rioting* by Martin Kettle in *The Guardian* 13th April
2001 © The Guardian 2001. Reprinted by permission of Guardian
Newspapers Limited; Letter from *Private lives* from *The Guardian*
13th April 2001 © The Guardian 2001. Reprinted by permission of
Guardian Newspapers Limited; Adapted text from *The latest look
involves addition and subtraction* from Your Life 21st May 2001.
Reprinted by permission; Extract from
Whole latte shakin by Christine Whitehouse from *Time
International* 9th April 2001 © 2001 Time Inc. Reprinted by
permission; *Welcome back cat* from *The Greenwich Mercury* 28th
March 2001. Reprinted by permission of the publishers South London
and Mercury Group.
The authors and publishers would like to thank the following for
permission to reproduce the following photographic material: Corbis
pp 10 (Walter Smith), 16 (David Bartruff), 28 (Neal Preston), 32
(Angelo Hornak), 52 (Eye Ubiquitous); Empics p22; FPG
International p40; Hulton Archive p31; Popperfoto p48 (Jonathan
Evans –Reuters); Michael Thomas p8.

Printed in Thailand.

2012 2011 2010 2009 2008
12   11   10   9   8